THE JOURNAL OF
A COUNTRY PARISH

The Journal of
A Country Parish

Robin Page

with illustrations by Fiona Silver

Oxford   New York
OXFORD UNIVERSITY PRESS
1986

Oxford University Press, Walton Street, Oxford OX2 6DP
Oxford New York Toronto
Delhi Bombay Calcutta Madras Karachi
Kuala Lumpur Singapore Hong Kong Tokyo
Nairobi Dar es Salaam Cape Town
Melbourne Auckland

and associated companies in
Beirut Berlin Ibadan Nicosia

Oxford is a trade mark of Oxford University Press

First published 1980 by Davis-Poynter Limited
First issued as an Oxford University Press paperback 1986

British Library Cataloguing in Publication Data
Page, Robin
The journal of a country parish.
1. Country life—England—Cambridgeshire
2. Cambridgeshire—Social life and customs
I. Title
942.6'50857'0924 DA670.C
ISBN 0-19-281893-7

Library of Congress Cataloging in Publication Data
Page, Robin, 1943–
The journal of a country parish.
(Oxford paperbacks)
Includes index.
1. Cambridgeshire—Description and travel.
2. Cambridgeshire—Social life and customs. 3. Country
life—England—Cambridgeshire. 4. Page, Robin,
1943– —Diaries. I. Title.
DA670.C2P33 1986 942.6'5 85-25975
ISBN 0-19-281893-7 (pbk.)

Printed in Great Britain by
The Guernsey Press Co. Ltd.
Guernsey, Channel Islands

Contents

Acknowledgements

I would like to thank all those who helped me with this book, both knowingly and unknowingly. In particular I would like to thank members of my family, who knew that even in times of stress or difficulty they would probably end up 'in print', and also to the many people in the parish, and those who visited the farm, most of whom had no idea that an account of village life was being kept.

I am also very grateful to Charlie Disbrey for letting me quote his delightful Christmas poem.

Introduction

❧

THE AIM OF THIS BOOK is simply to record the life of a country parish through the course of a single year. Although it is the parish in which I live, the moods, feelings and changes of season could belong to virtually any village in the British Isles. Observation has been made easier by the fact that during the year I worked as 'part-time village postman', which meant cycling around part of the parish for one and a half hours early each morning, six days a week. Apart from brief excursions to see deer, otters, falcons, and rocky coastal islands, I stayed in and around the area most of the time.

Each month I walked the fields and meadows, and watched life on the farm and in the village streets. Often I took my dogs along with me, for with their combined noses, little of interest escaped notice. Fiona Silver who drew the illustrations also spent much time taking in the parish year. Consequently in words and drawings we have recorded some of the beauties and some of the anxieties of country life; the old traditions, the still-living wisdom of country lore, the humour, the anguish, and the more obvious social and physical changes that intrude ever further into the rural way of life. In addition we have tried to show some of the wildflowers and wild creatures that continue to come and go with the ebb and flow of day and night, heat and cold, summer and winter. Each chapter begins with a few lines of poetry by John Clare the nineteenth century 'peasant poet', for many of his poems show some of the links with the past that can still be seen and felt today.

Many people yearn for the countryside and country living, but few have the pleasure or the opportunity of fulfilling their dreams. Those who do are often driven so hard by social and financial pressures that they know and see little of the life going on around them; yet they too exert influences and attitudes that change the parishes in which they live.

INTRODUCTION

In capturing the passage of a village year it is hoped that some of those who read this Journal, will feel and see the realities of country life, and in so doing, perhaps they will also understand.

January

Withering and keen the winter comes
While comfort flyes to close shut rooms
And sees the snow in feathers pass
Winnowing by the window glass

JANUARY STARTED DULL, but it soon lived up to its reputation for: 'Winter weather and women's thoughts often
change'. In the first week gales came and one morning sheet
lightning and a sudden clap of thunder heralded a violent storm.
Hail bounced over the lawn and then rain sluiced down. This is
said to be a bad omen, for:

Winter thunder, summer hunger

However some country people say:

Winter thunder, a summer's wonder

which is either promising a good summer, or just expressing surprise at out of season thunder.

Open skies and frost followed, and they in turn changed to
freezing fog. At dawn on the ninth a vivid rainbow appeared in
the western sky, and, sure enough, rain came, proving the
wisdom of:

A rainbow at night, fair weather in sight,
A rainbow at morn, fair weather all gorn.

The explanation for this piece of weather-lore is quite simple, for
rainbows appear when the sun shines into rain. Consequently in

the morning, the eastern sun shines into the clouds and rain of the west, and as most of our rain comes from the west, a wet day is likely. In the evening when a rainbow appears, the sun shines from the western sky, with rain in the east indicating that the bad weather has almost past.

After the gales, frost, and rain, cold variable weather continued with periodic freezes and thaws, and there was quite a hard frost on the thirteenth, St Hilary's Day, which is by repute the coldest day of the year. Even stronger gales then accompanied snow from the north, snapping off trees and tearing down weakened

bridge of willow over the brook

limbs and branches, one of which formed an attractive bridge of willow over the brook. Several years ago it would have gradually fallen into the brook itself, to form a natural dam, giving the brook character and depth. Now, due to the work of the local Water Authority, the brook has been changed into little more than an efficient ditch, and the new natural arch will not be allowed to stay for long. Beside the brook, willow branches were down. It was as if the trees had grown resistant to the usual winds from the south and west, but the gales from the north found new weaknesses and many trees and branches crashed down.

The old elm tree where I found my first fox cub, in a hole in the trunk, snapped at ground level, and in the spinney there were casualties of elm, ash and hawthorn. Even branches of ivy had been torn from their hold and ripped off, showing the strength of the wind.

Others, too, suffered during the month, but not because of the wind or the cold. On a freezing, misty Sunday the dogs dived into a hedge, and after a short squeal, Tinker emerged crushing the body of a rabbit between her teeth. She is the oldest and wisest of the dogs, a labrador with a small amount of alsation blood, and she kills quickly. The rabbit had swollen eyes with raw closed lids, for it had myxomatosis, and death must have been a release. It was the first affected rabbit I had seen for eighteen months, but when 'mexy' strikes many animals die and the dogs kill those they find, or munch up the bones of old carcasses; although a greater percentage of the rabbits survive than when the disease was first introduced, I always feel sadness and anger when I see it, for it was deliberately developed and spread by Man. Some rabbits appear to remain immune and alert, however, and Foss the border collie, the fastest of the dogs, chases them enthusiastically, without success.

Many birds were affected by the cold, the pheasants sat tighter in the fields, and twice Foss was within inches of seizing hen birds as they delayed take-off. Occasionally a pheasant is seen without its long tail feathers and it is said that these are the birds that have narrowly escaped the jaws of a fox. Around the house fieldfares and redwings were busy in the garden, and in two days fieldfares stripped an old lady's holly tree of all its berries, except for about a dozen at the very ends of the branches. But the cold did not last and was finally broken by rain during the night, which some countrymen call 'a duck's frost'.

On 25th January it is said that:

> *If St Paul's Day be fair and clear,*
> *Then it betides a happy year.*

Almost uncannily the day was fair and clear, from dusk to dawn, although it was hemmed in by two days that were cold, wet, and miserable.

The month ended spectacularly. As dawn came, a late hard frost arrived; it felt almost as if every breath of warmth was being sucked upwards into an icy vacuum. As the sky reddened it seemed to get even colder; the puddles iced over and soon the whole morning sky was a brilliant red. By eleven o'clock it was milder and it had started to rain:

Red sky in the morning, shepherd's warning.

Although winter is generally considered to be a dead season, yet there is life and activity to be seen in every month. One morning I found violets already on flower in a sheltered garden, and aconites too were opening. They are attractive little flowers, which push up with the new year to show that the season is turning towards spring. If the earth is eased away, the yellow, tightly packed

aconites

petals can even be seen underground, and once up, with the frill formed by their leaf-like bracts, each one looks like a small choirboy, or tudor courtier. with a ruff of green; then, as the flowers fade, so the leaves grow and fan out.

In fact it is surprising just how many flowers can be found in January, and this year groundsel, chickweed, speedwell, red-deadnettle and even one or two daisies were all out during the month. It is surprising too, just how much beauty is missed; for many years I have walked or ridden my bicycle past a small garden, several times each week, but for the first time this year I noticed winter heliotrope flowering at the base of the hedge. It is an interesting plant, rather like small butterbur; originally it was brought into the country as an ornamental flower, but now it is quite wild in many areas. From among its large leaves single stems emerge with small whitish flowers at the top, and the smell is reminiscent of almonds, or cherry pie.

If the weather holds, work can still be done on the land, and Plough Monday is the first Monday after old Christmas Day, 6th January. In bygone days it was hoped that all the ploughing would be finished by that date, which, at a time of real horse-power must have meant much hard work. This year Plough Monday fell on 9th January and Father was busy trying to finish the last of the ploughing; the land was wet and heavy and he could only use two furrows. There is something oddly satisfying about ploughing, gained from the way in which the soil is turned over in long straight lines. The feelings must be similar to those experienced by fishermen as they head for port on a fixed course. The lapwings appreciated the opportunities offered to them by the work of the plough, and fed steadily. When they flew, smaller, faster birds got up with them, showing the presence of a few golden plovers. Later in the day rain came, the clay got heavier and ploughing was abandoned.

With livestock, winter can be difficult, for there is always feeding, milking, or 'mucking out' to be done. It can be hard, cold and heavy work, carrying buckets, food, bales of hay and straw, and using pitch-forks and shovels, seven days a week. We are the only farm for several miles now that retains dairy cattle, and with our fields of grass and high hedges, our land is like a small island surrounded by comparatively tree-less tracts of arable prairie. If people think that we are backward, then we are not sorry.

The vet is a regular caller. On one damp afternoon he had to vaccinate calves against Johne's disease; it is a terrible wasting illness which causes the animal gradually to die in a never ending stream of almost liquid dung. At one time its threat was a constant worry, and at regular intervals cows would have to be loaded up for slaughter before they became worse. Now vaccinations are successful, and represent an advance that saves much anxiety, suffering and money.

The vet is a Welshman named Williams, who works with Robert, a younger vet from the Lake district; for no apparent reason one is always called by his surname, and the other by his Christian name. They are both amusing and patient men; they have to be, for sick animals cannot talk, and some of the conditions in which they work would make other men join unions. But secretly, I suspect, they both regret the decline in mixed farming and the loss of the dairy herds, for most of their work now involves cats, dogs, and even goldfish, and they seem to welcome the opportunity to put their five years of training to better use.

The last calf Williams had to inject was a climber, and although only two days old, it had already climbed over the bales of hay which made a temporary pen with walls five feet high. 'You call this a climber', he said, 'You should have seen the one I had once. A young cow climbed up onto the flat top of a stack of bales. "Don't move or the bloody thing will fall off", the farmer cried, going white. But he was too late for it jumped over the edge and disappeared from sight. We ran round the corner expecting to find a broken hip at least, but it just shook itself, bucked, and walked off. It was too silly to land on its head, and to make it more amazing it had landed on concrete. They should have shown it on television in that series about the life of a young country vet. You should see all the complaints they have from nice people who eat meat and drink milk, just because of a brief shot of the vet with his arm up the arse of a cow. Oh its much too disgusting and bad for the children; they should show them what we really do.'

The calf was injected without further mountaineering and Williams finished his visit by looking at Tinker. She views him with distrust, although she has never been ill or injured sufficiently for treatment, yet she seems to know his function. He found a few small lumps near her nipples that he will have to check in six weeks time. She has been a fine old dog, and it will be sad if this is the beginning of the end.

Two days later the vet was needed again, but there was no time to contact him. As father drove the cows out of the yard for milking, he noticed a pulsating fountain of blood coming from the hind legs of one of the heifers. It had cut an artery, just above the hoof, and was in need of urgent treatment. Fortunately Rachael, my youngest sister, a nurse, was at home; the heifer was driven into the milking bale and she put her thumb over the cut to stop the bleeding. While disinfectant was being found the frightened animal kicked out, spraying blood in all directions, and the anti-kick bar had to be applied. It is a simple contraption, rather like a pair of handlebars, with one end going over the heifer's back, and the other sticking into its flank, so that discomfort is caused by any movement. The wound was bathed and blocked up with cotton wool. It was then tied up with an old crêpe bandage and kept in place with baler twine. By the time Williams arrived the job was done; he commended the effort and gave an injection to aid coagulation of the blood. Even walking about in the yard would not be too bad for the injury, as 'cow-muck' is considered to be anti-septic by some farmers and it can be used for a variety of complaints including baldness, skin trouble, and cuts.

The injury to the cow was a reminder of the transience of life. On this occasion however, because of prompt action and good fortune, the animal and three hundred pounds were saved. Sometimes things do not work out so well.

Although they make much work, it is pleasant having cattle on the farm, for cows are attractive animals, with large liquid eyes and enquiring flapping ears. It is interesting too, for despite centuries of domestication, they still show flashes of behaviour remarkably similar to that of their distant relatives, wild deer.

On the farm, even during the coldest weather, some of the young heifers and bullocks remained in the meadows along the brook. During the day of snow and galeforce winds, I decided to go and check to make sure that they were alright. The snow was being blown horizontally across the road and the wind made my cheeks burn with cold. Down by the brook, birds were reluctant to fly and fieldfares and blackbirds sought refuge in the under-growth. Even the dogs stayed close to me, and had lost their usual enthusiasm for hunting. Snow stuck to teasels, and on their wind-ward side the trees were plastered with white. The only respite came along one hedge where brambles gave added insulation against the wind. The young cattle were standing near a hedge with their rear ends to the wind. They looked forlorn and re-minded me of the old saying: 'Winter and wedlock tame man and beast.' But it was clearly the best position for them, with their tails fitting perfectly for warmth and their large ears keeping the snow from their eyes. Strangely, even the heifer without a tail stood in exactly the same way, with her backside icily exposed. She was born without a tail, so the old proverb of 'The cow knows not what her tail is worth till she has lost it', is not really appropriate. She was the first such calf that either the vet or the inseminator had seen; an oddity that defied explanation. Despite her loss however, she seems content, and she is only at a disadvantage during icy winds, and in the summer when the flies are biting.

Back by the warmth of our open log fire, I couldn't get the heifer and its icy aspect out of my mind, for it seemed to confirm the simple fact that all cows are not born equal. Some are strong, some are weak, some are large, some are small, and in this case, some are incomplete. Similarly when they mature they have vastly differing temperaments, yet following birth, they are all treated identically. They are allowed to suckle the first bisnings* from their mother, before it thins and becomes normal milk, and then they are taken away and fed on powdered milk, until they are old enough for solids and hay. But by the time they have their calves, they have all acquired individuality. It is usually the same cow that finds the gap in hedges and fences, and leads the others through into the corn; some discover how to let themselves out of the milking bale; some are patient, others are indifferent; some kick and some remain calm. Each breed too has its own characteristics, and even the milk of Friesians and Jerseys differ, for Jersey milk contains much more cream.

---

*Beestings

The observations are simple, yet their implications are considerable, especially if applied to people, for they would show differences of type and temperament, caused through a mixture of background, race, and genetics. Such considerations are, of course, almost blasphemy in respectable political circles, for men from Abraham Lincoln to Karl Marx have proclaimed that 'all men are born equal'. Consequently one of the most favoured

political slogans is also one of the most inaccurate, for if cows are born unequal, then it is more than likely that men and women are too. And so, from gazing into the backside of a cow comes simple political truth.

One of the reasons why I like January is because it is the month of the wild fox, when foxes can often be seen and heard and when mating normally takes place. Twice while out with the dogs I saw a large fox, in fine condition, with a white tip to its tail, down in the brook meadows. On the first occasion it crossed the middle of the field, but the dogs did not see it, as they were too busy chasing rabbits. The second time they set off in brief pursuit, but the fox quickly lost them.

The presence of foxes is also shown by the clear fox path that winds up to our deep-litter shed, and from the clarity of the track it must be used on most nights. This was confirmed with the arrival of snow, for fox tracks were clearly visible, as they were in many of the meadows. Several nights too, I heard foxes barking, and one was very close to the farm. The bark of a fox is far different from that of a dog, being shorter and more mournful; indeed on a moonlit night it has an extremely eerie quality. Foxes were heard all around the village during the month, and on several nights one could be heard in fields next to the High Street.

Although fox activity is obvious to those interested in country life, few people have actually seen foxes mate and there is much debate as to whether foxes are promiscuous or monogamous, and whether they mate like dogs. On a cold damp morning, early in the month, the farmer who farms close to the rifle range, on the other side of the parish, noticed a fox walking alongside a hedge close to his farm. It disappeared briefly, but quickly re-emerged and began to walk towards the middle of the field. Suddenly another fox came from the hedge and followed about fifteen yards behind. The tails of both animals were twitching from side to side, almost like a slow motion wag. Once in the middle, the vixen stopped and the dog approached and mounted her. Over the years the farmer had lost a lot of poultry and he ran for his rifle. When he returned the pair were 'knotted', back to back like dogs, and from a range of two hundred and fifty yards he let fly. 'You should have seen them. They didn't know whether they were coming or going. It took them about ten seconds to separate, a bit quicker than dogs, and they were gone.' He is a reliable man and his sighting of foxes locked in passion must be almost unique.

For some years I have wanted my pet vixen to breed, in order to see the family life of a fox at close quarters. At one time I had a young dog fox with her, but he escaped, and I have always refrained from staking her out in January, or whenever she seems to be on heat, to avoid attacks by roaming dogs. In any case breeding is not straightforward, for vixens have been known to come into season as early as October and as late as April, and once on heat they can only be successfully mated during a crucial period of between two and four days.

By a strange coincidence, a few months ago, I discovered two more tame foxes in the next village. They are fine animals, well looked after, and fed on a diet of deep frozen rats; they were found as cubs in Wales and rescued from motorway construction. The dog is large and placid, named Botoch, the Gaelic for old man, and the vixen is more temperamental and called Creoch, or thief. When Rusty was introduced into their cage it was not known how they would all react, for foxes, like most animals, are very territorial.

At first, whenever Rusty approached either of the other two, their ears would go flat and back, and with their mouths open they would make strange threatening noises, like a cross between a growl and a squeal, almost coughed out. On one occasion Rusty was bitten sharply across the nose by the other vixen, but mainly there were just threats. Another time, Botoch arched his back, and with his brush aloft, he rubbed against the wire mesh as if he was scenting to assert his authority, but then he disappeared inside his box. Rusty spent most of her time under a sawn-up section of hollow tree trunk, but gradually the swearing and displaying declined, until by the end of the month they were all living together quite peacefully. Rusty and Botoch even slept together, but unfortunately they did nothing more than sleep. On returning to the farm she was very excited and pulled so hard on her lead that I let her go. She ran straight back to her shed and wagged her brush, wanting to play. The stay had not unsettled her, but neither had it given her cubs.

The village church, like many others in the area, dates back to the eleventh century, and has a fine square tower with battlements at the top. It can be seen from most parts of the parish and at one time it was important in the life of the village. Now some services are very sparsely attended, but on the last Sunday of the month it was packed for the farewell service of the vicar, who was retiring after nine years in the village. Like all vicars, he was viewed in a variety of ways by different people; he was considered to be aloof, friendly, too conservative, too liberal, like-able and a snob. In much the same way, as soon as a new man is installed, the old vicar's reputation will improve steadily, until he seems almost like a latter-day saint.

The church is beautiful, and as the service went on it was impossible not to compare the craftsmanship and skill that went into its construction with the mass-produced and processed skills of today. It contains the work of builders, carpenters, wood-carvers, stonemasons, and artists, and the skill and pride which worked their hands still shows. The walls were made from field stones and rubble, held in by cement. The pulpit was built in 1635. There is an elaborately carved wooden screen. The windows in the chancel are of stained glass, and even the wooden leaves on the choir stalls show both a simple beauty and an artist's eye. With their old hand tools and practised skills they created a building of simplicity and beauty which is a tribute to their age. By contrast, the Silver Jubilee plinth, erected near the village pond, bears witness to modern-day tastes and teaching, for it looks like an ornamental fire hydrant.

It was the wall paintings that provided the vicar with his final difficulty, for on some of the walls are fourteenth-century paint-ings denoting an assortment of saints. Over recent years they have faded fast, and in one of his parish letters the vicar wrote: 'On a bright day, and with the help of binoculars, it is still possible to see much of the detail of these old paintings.' Consequently he, and the Parochial Church Council, decided on costly restoration, in stages. He met with enthusiastic support from some who wanted to conserve part of our 'national heri-tage', and hostility from others, who seemed to think that the money could be better spent saving the rest of the world from starvation. The vicar won, and he proudly mentioned the first restored picture in his farewell message.

As the congregation left in the rain, the gargoyles at the corner of the tower showered them with water from the roof. Tea, sandwiches and cakes were served in large quantities in the school, and belatedly people smiled. It was announced that £246 had been raised as a parting gift, and the vicar was presented with a model garden shed to remind him of the occasion, even after the real one had been erected at the bottom of his new garden.

February

The snow is gone from cottage tops
The thatch moss glows in brighter green
And eyes in quick succession drops
Where grinning icicles once hath been

THE SECOND OF FEBRUARY is Candlemas Day, and it is said that:

If Candlemas be fair and bright,
Winter'll have another flight,
But if Candlemas Day be clouds and rain,
Winter is gone and will not come again.

The day was cold and wet, which was disappointing, for according to tradition it would mean another winter without skating. By the next morning however, it seemed that the old forecast might be wrong, for as the sun came up, and with the moon still bright, it froze hard. Indeed the early morning frost was so severe that starlings were able to land on the ice covering a large field puddle. By the old parish osier bed, alongside the brook, about twenty pheasants fed and sunned themselves, and somehow, they seemed to know that the shooting season had just finished.

The fourth was also unusual, for although it rained almost continuously, Spring seemed to be in the air. There was a definite dawn chorus, the first of the year, with blackbirds, thrushes, robins, great-tits, wrens and skylarks, all singing clearly; two sparrows mated in a lilac bush; one of the farmyard geese laid her first egg of the year, and a few snowdrops opened. Nothing was different to human ears and eyes, but to those more sensitive and responsive a new season could be discerned and had already begun.

I became aware too of something that I had not heard for several years; it was the drumming of a woodpecker. The sound of rapid-fire carpentry carried from a large garden, filled with old trees including dead elms and ancient ashes. With each new burst I scanned the trees but could locate no bird. I hoped that such vigorous activity would show the return to the parish of the green-woodpecker, a bird that has been absent since the hard winter of 1962-1963. Eventually I saw movement, halfway up a trunk, but it seemed far too small for a woodpecker. My doubts quickly went, for a renewed burst of drumming rattled out as its bill hammered into the bark with great power. It was a lesser-spotted woodpecker, a tiny bird, only the size of a sparrow, with

lesser-spotted woodpecker

the typical undulating flight of all woodpeckers. It continued working busily and sporadically and stayed in the garden, apparently alone, for several days.

More rain followed and the brook overflowed part of its banks for a few brief hours; it was certainly a case of 'February fill dyke'. Many of the birds appreciated the wet however; there were snipe in the fields, several groups of mallard searched in the puddles and grass of Warners Corner, and groups of golden plovers were often seen wheeling and gliding in unison before landing on ploughed land. From the number of rabbits in the hedges it was clear that many had been flooded out of their burrows, and they would have to rely on their speed and camouflage for survival. Their chances were slightly increased by the death of a fox, for its body lay by the roadside where it had been knocked over by a car.

Half way through the month, snow and ice returned, and at night the temperature fell and the cold intensified, for 'as the days lengthen, so the cold strengthens'. Where a spring gushed into the brook large icicles formed, but each morning the temperature crept up to above freezing, making branches and roofs drip steadily. Ice covered the ponds and two large puddles on a field of winter wheat, and skates were taken out in readiness, but the ice just would not bear. Before the work of the Water Authority, the brook would have flooded the nearby grass meadows with a few inches of still water, and skating would have been possible. Consequently the skating tradition of the area is gradually dying. On the brook itself only a few fingers of ice formed along the edges, with no hope of linking across the fast flow.

The wind then veered to the east, 'putting a real edge on it', and the snow lingered by the hedgerows as if 'waiting for more'. Along sections of the brook it actually drove waves against the current, giving it the odd appearance of flowing backwards. The cold had its compensations however, for the air felt clean, and redwings came into the garden, seemingly without fear. They worked among the dead weeds in front of the kitchen window, moving and pulling on stems as they searched for seeds and insects. They are pretty thrushlike birds and welcome visitors of winter.

About one more night of frost was needed for skating when the thaw came. It came too in an unusual way, as rain, which as soon as it landed froze, forming a treacherous covering of black ice over paths and lawns. Even trees were covered and the slender branches of the weeping willow in the garden rattled in the breeze, sounding like a curtain of glass beads. But then the temperature rose and the real thaw came with dripping, and flowing ditches.

But despite the coolness of the winter, the approach of spring could still be seen and felt. In sheltered ditches the first leaves of willowherb pushed upwards and cuckoo pint emerged under the protection of the elms in the 'jungle', a wild meadow by the brook. The first crocuses flowered and the hazel catkins loosened to show where nuts might be found in the autumn. On the last day

hazel catkins

of the month a wren sang and displayed by the coal shed, ignoring my presence. It perched about a foot away from my head with its wings opening and quivering, its tail erect, and its feathers so clearly and distinctly marked that it looked far too fragile to be real.

Because of the rain most of the farmwork was routine; looking after the livestock, cleaning out sheds and grinding corn, but despite this, Williams had to come again, for the unpleasant task of de-horning the young cattle. Father, brother John, and Charlie, a retired signalman who hobbles as he helps, were all in attendance. The cattle were driven one by one into a do-it-yourself crush, and the horns were cut off with a contraption like a glorified cheese wire. Williams gave each one a local anaesthetic, and as father held the head, with a finger firmly placed up each nostril, John sawed with the wire. When a horn fell a fountain of blood usually shot upwards, showing that a small artery had been nicked, and a young cow with two fountains of blood spurting from its head made a bizarre sight. The bleeding quickly stopped however, and as the heap of horns grew bigger, so the dogs became interested in the activity. The first to arrive was Nellie, a biological oddity, for although her brothers and sisters looked like labradors, she was always smaller and longer, and now she looks anything but labrador; indeed, it seems almost as if the one litter had two fathers. To add to her misfortune she lost an eye in an argument with a cat, and 'Nellie' developed from Nelson. To human nostrils the smell of severed horn is rather like that of old socks, but to Nellie it was obviously quite different. After trying to chew a stolen horn, she gave up, and buried it carefully in a pile of sand for later use. 'Now look what she's done', Williams objected, 'when I want to know how many cows we've done, I count the horns and divide by two; now we'll have to count all the legs and divide by four. You should have seen the sight when I started as a young vet. I managed to get the wire round an ear as well as a horn. Yet this old bloke lent against the fence, watching carefully, and when I had almost finished he casually said: "What do you want to go and cut its ear off for?" The silly old bugger; it needed thirty-two stitches to sew it back on again, and he had just stood and watched.'

After dinner all the dogs had taken to horn burying and there were just four left.

One of the sounds of the month was that made by mechanical chain saws. The bridge of willow was quickly cut into sections and heaped onto the bank, and much wood clearing and hedging took place. At one time February was regarded as the month for hedging, when the hawthorn was cut, trimmed and layed to make cattle proof field boundaries. It was a craft demanding knowledge, skill and care, but as few hedges are now required it has almost died out. Today hedges are hacked and ripped by high-powered flail mowers, with whirling arms of insensitive metal. The limbs and branches are torn, beaten and severed, and the hedge is left looking harsh and humiliated. The care has gone, and the lack of feeling and the mechanical process both leave their mark. Hedging is now simply a job to fill in time when there is nothing else to do; hedges serve no purpose and their aesthetic value is often lost among balance sheets and a desire for 'tidy' fields. A hired flail mower came on to the farm for the first time, to get the job done quickly. In two days three long hedges were halved in size, and the short strip of hedge which father wanted to lay in the old way, to practice his skill, was left for another year.

With central heating and electric fires, much wind-fall wood is now just heaped up and left to rot; a waste that a few years ago would never have been allowed, for trees supplied many local needs. Among the most important was willow, and those growing along the brook were pollarded or 'doddled', and used for sheep hurdles. The now overgrown osier bed provided wands of willow for basket making, and a small group of trees was planted for cricket bats. In addition, willow trees were found useful for fencing posts and thatching spits, and as willow grows and regrows quickly, it was said that: 'The willow will buy a horse before the oak will pay for a saddle.' Now the old pollard willows are never cut, and the top heavy trees are felled only by the wind.

Ash was another tree deliberately planted in hedgerows for its wood, and some people consider it to be even stronger than oak. It was particularly favoured for axe, hoe and fork handles. It is a pleasant wood with the feeling of strength in its smooth hard grain. Elms too, were doddled locally, but their wood is less reliable because it rots quite quickly: 'That's why they were used for coffins, to allow the worms through quicker.'

We still burn wood on open fires during the winter and the chain-saw was often in action during the month. Much sweat is saved as the engine races and it is a peculiarly satisfying feeling to cut through wood. It can be dangerous however, and one brief lapse in concentration ruined a pair of my wellington boots, but fortunately no real harm was done. Because of its speed and power, jobs that once took days now take a few hours, and in a leisurely afternoon a large dead silver birch, that had died of a fungus disease, was taken down in the garden and sawn into logs. Once the branches and trunk had been cut into sections, then the felling-axe was used to split them into smaller and more usable logs, and again the action of splitting logs with an axe is soothing and enjoyable. If only the axe, the bow saw, and the large cross-cut saw, that now hangs unused in the old granary, had been used, the task of sawing would have been very tedious and laborious, and so 'progress' has some favourable aspects.

We burn any wood that becomes available, and despite the saying that 'Green elm burns like the churchyard sod, and its flame is just as cold,' we even use elm. Live elm is very difficult to burn, but logs from trees that have died of Dutch Elm Disease make good fires, although sometimes they have to be split several times, using large cast iron wedges and a seven-pound hammer. The birch logs also went well and for several years we have used much willow. Willow wood is often under-rated as a fuel because when green it spits, sending sparks and embers flying in all directions. But if left a year to dry out, it burns reasonably well, with few fire hazards. Ash is again one of the most useful woods and it is said that 'Ash dry or ash green, makes a fire fit for a queen.' Some of the best but scarcest logs come from old apple, plum, and pear trees, for although not smelling as sweet as their blossom, their logs give out a pleasant smoky aroma. There is no doubt that log fires are the most comforting and cheering form of winter warmth. They are certainly more pleasant than radiators and the arid airlessness found in rooms warmed by central heating.

When I was cycling along the High Street one morning I was stopped by one of the few villagers who still works on the land; he told me of a pair of otters that had been living in a neighbouring parish for several months. It was good news, for otters have been scarce for many years because of pollution, disturbance, and the way in which our rivers, brooks, and streams have been denuded of cover.

I made two journeys to walk along the length of river concerned. The first was after much rain, and although the water had fallen by two feet, it was still high and flowing fast. The river is meandering and wide, and the brook flows into it a mile down-stream. A clear line of silt showed just how high the level had been and a large roach lay marooned in the mud. It was only just alive, and apart from a slightly damaged mouth it looked in fine condition. It could have been struck by a piece of wood, or float-ing rubbish, but how it had become stranded above the falling water line was not clear.

Despite efforts to revive it in the water, the fish almost certainly died. Further along, pied and grey wagtails flitted from side to side among the high water debris, which included the almost perfect empty shell of a fresh water mussel. A moorhen ran splashing along the surface to cover, and the footprints of a heron disappeared deep into the water; but there were no signs of otters.

On the second visit the water level had fallen considerably, and near the arched road bridge, where the bed is stony and the flow is fast, it looked almost like a highland stream instead of a lowland river, and even a dipper would not have been out of place. Walking downstream the depth increased and the flow slowed; suddenly something dived beneath the surface, but from the splash and the line of bubbles it was probably a moorhen. A heron watched me from the middle of a field, and when it took off its legs trailed out behind as it flew slowly away. Where the river curved, three teal sprang up from the water, quickly and easily; they are attractive fast flying little ducks and 'a spring of teal' is a most fitting description.

The fields along one bank are some of the few remaining water meadows of old grass in the area. They are particularly favoured by golden plovers, and three or four hundred were dotted about in small groups. Golden plovers are beautiful birds, smaller than lapwings, with fast wingbeats and the narrow curved wings of true waders. They fly in complete unison and their plaintive piping calls are evocative of wild lonely places. It was cold, and they were not keen to fly; as a result some allowed me to get within thirty yards of them, closer than I had ever been before, and they looked really 'golden' in the rays of the setting sun.

Again there were no signs of otters, and even if they were still there, it seemed likely that their stay would soon be coming to an end. Beyond the point where the river merged with another, and close to where the brook flows in, the foundations of a new motorway bridge were being driven into the clay. There were earth movers, lorries, reinforced steel and general commotion. Each time the pile-driver crashed down on metal, it sounded like the simple bell of a far off Spanish church, summoning its worshippers to praise God. The new symbols of progress have their worshippers too, but the God has changed.

Although otters do not seem to have ventured into the parish, there were other visitors, who were far less welcome. At one time genuine gypsies with their horses, caravans, dogs and children would regularly pass through, but they have now been replaced by didecoys; itinerant landworkers, scrap merchants and general scavengers who travel about in vans, pick-up trucks, and who live in caravans. For several weeks one such family had been living in mud and squalor in an old driftway, between farm fields, just outside the village.

A few years ago the drift was wedged in with high hedges, and it was like a sheltered island of peace and tranquillity, leading to the top of a low hill. In summer, wildflowers and grasses grew in profusion, the hedges held in the heat, and farm trailers left a layer of drifting dust in the air. Now the hedges have been cut to a fraction of their former size, and in winter the entrance is rutted and awash with mud. Along half its length the drift is littered with rusting metal, empty beer cans, broken milk bottles, used toilet paper, and squattings of human dung.

As I approached one afternoon, even the dogs seemed apprehensive at the sight. When a large alsation and a scruffy small terrier appeared from one of the caravans, Nellie fled yelping away, with the two dogs in close pursuit. Tinker went through the hedge and into the field, looking for somewhere cleaner. The owner, Mr Smith, claimed that he was of gypsy descent. It was difficult to tell his age through his grime and his rotting teeth which stuck out at differing angles, like those of a ragged toothed shark: his hands were covered with oil, and his clothes shone with dirt. The family of eight were living in two caravans and comprised his wife, a wrinkled woman looking far older than her age, two large sons, three younger children, and a small curly-haired girl whose griminess was matched by her stickiness. Mr Smith said that every morning they had to walk over half a mile to fetch water in cans on an old pram; they had no van, and relied on friends to move them. Despite the signs of scrap dealing, Mr Smith claimed that he wasn't working, and that he was unlikely to work again before the summer. He said that in the old days 'I would pick spuds, single beet, and pick fruit in the summer, and go hedging and ditching in the winter, and the farmers would let us go in a quiet field out of the way. The farmers wanted us then, but there's nothing for us now only muddy drifts. Now if you wave to a farmer he looks the other way, but it's us gypsies who helped get them where they are. I'd like to go between walls now, I've had enough. I've got me name down for a house but don't suppose I'll get one.' His son disagreed: 'Houses are unhealthy. If I went into a house I couldn't guarantee that I would stay there.'

It was damp and cold talking to them, and even the two young game-fowl looked miserable as they stood hunched up by the door. 'A good fighting cock's worth between thirty to forty pounds,' the son went on, 'we fight them anywhere as long as the cops aren't around. A champion can fetch up to eighty pounds. Some get killed and some run away when they are beaten. You can get them to fight anywhere, even in mud like this if you like. We get little trouble from the police or the locals in this area; if people became too troublesome we would lump them.'

They stayed a few more days, and then they were gone, leaving behind the mud, broken glass, and the general smell and appearance of decay.

Other visitors came to the parish in hundreds and possibly even thousands, for the flocks of wood pigeons were larger than for several years. Their arrival was strange, for the previous year there were hardly any, leading to allegations that they had been 'over shot', and some people even called for a close season for pigeon-shooting. They need not have worried, for almost every day large flocks flew over, and in addition there was often a steady stream to favoured fields. On occasions some fields looked almost black with pigeons, and the invasion was said to have been caused by an influx of birds from Scandinavia. One morning a flock was so large that the rush of wingbeats could be clearly heard, and if disturbed while feeding, the birds would clatter noisily into the air. The fields most frequently visited by the pigeons were those sown with rape, and many of the small plants were almost stripped of their leaves. Those pigeons familiar with the area would fly directly to the fields and then perch in an old overgrown orchard, or in the spinney. Visiting or passing pigeons, or birds that had been shot at elsewhere, would fly over high, and on seeing the rape, they would tuck in their wings and fall out of the sky like wind thrown leaves. Several times men with guns hid in the orchard, with decoys placed out in the field, and shot throughout the day as the birds drifted in.

The effect of the shooting showed, for pigeons flying over the garden would accelerate and veer away on seeing human activity below. To me, pigeon shooting is not a pleasant task, for often the wounded birds are left where they fall, so that the 'flight' is not disturbed, and pigeons also seem to bleed more than other birds. Pigeon pie compensates, however, for both the crop damage and the suffering of shooting, and the warm smell of a winter kitchen as pigeon, crust, and gravy cook together is one of the season's pleasant memories.

Pigeon pie is simple to cook and four people can eat well off two birds. The pigeons should first be plucked and drawn, (although some people simply cut out the breasts and throw the rest away) and simmered gently with onions until they are tender. They should then be removed from the liquid and the meat cut off and put into a pie dish lined with pastry. The liquid can then be thickened with a tablespoonful of flour and seasoning, and poured over the meat.

The short crust pastry is made by mixing eight ounces of self-raising flour and four ounces of lard. The sides of the pie dish are lined with half the pastry and the top is covered with the rest. It should be cooked in a hot oven, until the pastry is done, and eaten with vegetables. Many people insist that pigeon pie makes a better meal than the over-rated grouse.

Simmering marmalade is another February smell in many country homes and coincides with the arrival of boat loads of Spanish Seville oranges. Homemade marmalade was made originally to save money, as it was so much cheaper than that available in shops. Electric mixers and shredders are now used to save time, but many of the old recipes are still followed and have been handed down through several generations. One evening our kitchen was saturated with the sweet smell of oranges and sugar. The recipe was old and written on paper now brown with age, it read:

12 Seville oranges and two sweet oranges.

Cut them in halves and carefully remove all the pips. Slice through the oranges finely, and to every pound of fruit add three pints of cold water and allow to stand for twenty-four hours.

Place pips in a basin and cover with one of the above pints of water; put to swell for twenty-four hours, strain off and add juice to the fruit which has been standing the same length of time. The juice of two lemons is a great improvement. Boil the fruit for two hours before adding the sugar until tender. Allow it to cool and add one and a quarter pounds of sugar to each pound of pulp. Boil about three-quarters of an hour after adding the sugar, or until it jellies.

March

March month of 'many weathers' wildly comes
In hail and snow and rain and threatening hums
And floods: while often at his cottage door
The shepherd stands to hear the distant roar

ACCORDING TO THE OLD RHYME March either comes in like a 'lion', or like a 'lamb'. On this occasion however, it came in like neither, being dull and damp, but overall it lived up to its reputation of 'March many weathers', for it contained good weather and bad, warm days and cool, high winds and pleasant calms.

By the second week it was warm, with a succession of spring-like days, and I saw my first bumblebee of the year droning around in the sun; it must have been a queen, for like wasps, only the queens survive the winter. A hive of honey bees on the other hand can carry on for several years, and they too were out in the sun, working the crocuses, and packing the pollen baskets on their back legs with pollen.

The first common wild flowers were also to be found, with the Lesser Celandine flowering in roadside verges, lawns, and damp waste

lesser celandine

33

places. It is a beautiful little flower with brilliant yellow petals and dark green, fresh looking leaves, which make a vivid contrast to the still dormant plants of winter around them. As a child I always knew it as the 'Kingcup', because the flowers seemed to be so much finer than those of the Buttercup which appeared later. The difference was appreciated by Wordsworth too, and he praised their early beauty in poetry. Flowering Colts-foot also reflected the approach of spring and I came across a group of them unexpectedly on the bank of the brook. It was a dull, overcast day, and the bright yellow flowers looked cheering and reassuring; the brook bank was sheltered, and facing south, and

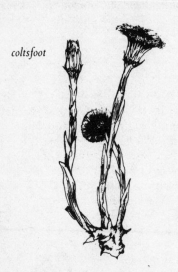

coltsfoot

the flowers stood erect on their leafless stems. In the osier bed the pussy willow was another to show the movement of the season, and when the sun shone the catkins streaked the trees with a sil-ver spray that was both soft to the eye and to the touch.

pussy willow

One afternoon along the brook meadows a woodcock flew by me at head height and only fifteen yards away. It was the first one I had ever seen in the parish, although they breed in small woods a few miles away. It flew at an almost leisurely pace and turned its head towards me as it passed; it too looked soft, with its delicate leaf-like markings showing clearly.

In the middle of the month cold returned with a north wind and two inches of snow to greet the early daffodils. It quickly thawed, but blustery showery weather prevented the land work from getting underway. Every evening a great-tit kept out of the cold in a neighbour's garden, for as dusk approached it would settle in a tree near an old water pump. Then, when all was clear, with no cats near, it would fly forward and with rapid aerial acrobatics it would disappear up the pump's spout for the night. The volume of birdsong gradually increased and a pair of wrens built a nest in a crack in the coal shed wall; they did not use it however, for wrens build several nests and evidently the coal shed site was not quite suitable.

Down at the Warners Corner earth it was not obvious whether a vixen was in residence for the birth of her litter. There were signs of rabbits all around, as usual, and although the dogs showed great interest in all the holes there was no way of finding out the identity of any of the occupants. If a vixen was present, then it was likely that her cubs would have been born during the month. At the entrance of a nearby rabbit 'stop', two small rabbits briefly peered out showing that in rabbit circles anyway the business of spring was already well under way.

More gales came, and one evening as the angry evening sun went down, the bark and the swelling buds of the garden weeping willow tree seemed to run with gold. Thunder brought hailstones bouncing over the lawn, proving the accuracy of 'Thunder in spring, cold it will bring', but then fine weather resumed.

Almost at the end of the month as I walked by the rifle range, a small flock of golden plovers flew over me. I clapped my hands, and in response they dived down in unison. In the days when plovers were considered a delicacy, it is said that countrymen would take advantage of this odd behaviour to bring the birds within shooting range. Along a ditch coltsfoot was growing in a great mass, on the spoil that had been thrown out during winter ditching, and it is another peculiarity of the plant that it loves bad or recently disturbed soil. On several ditch banks violets were flowering, purple and blue, and under one old, unkempt hedge they appeared in patches of pure white. Daffodils brightened the gardens and despite the cold and wet, primroses were better than they had been for several years.

It was frustrating on the farm, for as soon as the soil began to dry, rain returned and it seemed that 'April showers' had arrived a month early. It certainly emphasised the old saying: 'A peck of dust in March is worth a King's ransom', for dry soil was urgently needed. It was frustrating with the cattle too, for there was a tuberculosis test to organise and the usual crop of accidents occurred, including a small calf that broke its leg. Father tried to bind a splint across the break, but it would not hold and so the animal was taken to the veterinary school where the leg was pinned.

It was Williams who arrived to administer the test, which involved injecting tuberculin into the skin of every animal, to see if any reaction resulted later. It is undertaken every three years to ensure a disease free herd and to prevent TB from being trans- mitted through the milk to humans. It was hoped to complete the job in one morning session, but unfortunately the cows had other ideas. Each one had to be driven into the cattle crush, and once in, Charlie had to slide a long metal pipe in behind them to prevent retreat. One cow in its efforts to get out ended up on its back with its head stuck under the gate. Pulls and pushes were useless and it seemed that she would break her neck. Williams administered what he described as a friendly kick, 'she likes it really', but she was stuck fast until the gate was hurriedly levered from its hinges.

With running cattle and Charlie wielding his metal pipe it was dangerous and energetic exercise. When it was mentioned that an electric shock machine might be a good aid for driving awk- ward cattle, Charlie agreed: 'Cor that would make them jump. Do you remember when we had the pigs, that old boar having his oats one morning? While he was at it the sow liked it so much that she kept moving backwards until his balls touched the elec- tric wire. Gawd, he shot forward; he went in half an inch further than he had ever been before.' Williams had a better idea: 'You know what they used to do in the olden days with a stubborn horse or cow? They'd stick a hot potato up its arse. Charlie, you could be the one to carry the potato.'

Because of the running and chasing we had to break for dinner before all the animals had been tested. 'It's a good job we're not like those vets in the ministry', Williams informed us, 'I went to see one the other Friday afternoon. Everyone said that I would never see the big man as it was Poets' Day. Poets' Day? I asked. The answer was simple: "Piss off early tomorrow's Saturday".'

In the afternoon it was the turn of the young cattle. The Friesians were little trouble, but those crossed with a Murray-Grey, an Australian breed, ran, jumped, turned and wouldn't be driven, giving new candidates for the saying: 'Pigs, women and bees can never be turned'; indeed, at times it seemed as if they had been crossed with kangaroos. One burst through the side of the crush, nearly taking Charlie with it, but by that time he had done almost as much damage with his pipe, so the score was about even. Eventually the job was done, and when, a few days later, they were checked, the herd was found to be clear of any traces of TB.

After her test, one heavily pregnant cow got out and gave birth to her calf in the field. Although the bull calf was too heavy to carry home, and its legs were too wobbly to walk, there were no problems. By the next morning it had walked to the farm with its mother.

During a wet windy night another calving was not so easy. I looked around the farm just after midnight, to check the animals and the buildings, and found a cow lying down with her calf half out, as if she hadn't the strength to move it further. I pulled its front legs and it slid out easily, a fine fit calf, a Murray-Grey, that already seemed lively. The cow would not stand and I assumed that she had exhausted herself in labour and let her rest. Eventually I got her up, but she swayed drunkenly, staggered forwards a few paces and collapsed; it was a case of milk fever. Father joined me and we tried to get her to cleaner ground but she would not move. With a needle, a length of rubber tube, and a butterfly valve, calcium* was injected into her neck, which is the most

---

*Calcium Borogluconate.

effective way of treating the condition, and certainly better than the old method, which involved hanging afterbirth in a hawthorn tree. We then covered her with old sacks to keep her warm for the night and carried the still steaming calf, by its legs, upside down, into a small shed. At two o'clock, cold, wet, and filthy we returned to the farmhouse. By the evening of the next day, and after another pint of calcium, the cow had recovered and half a gallon of milk was taken from her for her calf. It had not drunk since birth, but it soon grasped the idea of sucking fingers, which were then lowered into a bucket containing the milk.

A few days later another freshly calved cow was down, but once more calcium quickly restored her. Nellie arrived on the scene, until the old cow moved towards her menacingly. The dogs know that cows with calves mean business, and even Foss keeps away. Tinker was the next to arrive, for she has a great appetite for afterbirth, as does John's dog, Tirra; it is strange how dogs are considered to be attractive by men, yet their digestive and sexual habits leave so much to be desired. Geese however, are much more reserved and discreet, and although a gosling hatched during the month, we did not see the gander do his duty; needless to say, Charlie was the one exception.

Over the years the animal population and the nature of the farm have changed. The change was emphasised to me when I found an old horseshoe in the field at the back of the farmhouse, just lying in the grass. Despite being shed by a working horse, no farm horse has plodded over the fields of the farm for about thirty years, and since cast, the shoe must have been ploughed in and out of the ground several times, yet it had remained unnoticed. At one time it was thought to be lucky to find a horseshoe, but I took it home simply because I was glad to find a reminder of a past age; an age which to many is still within living memory, although to most it is already part of distant history. But despite our motorised and 'civilised' times, horses continue to be remembered with affection on the farms, and for many generations Britain's economic and military strength depended on them.

Old men in the village remember riding them and working with them, and one of my grandfathers started his working life as a groom. Indeed horses continued to work some of the fields of the parish for several years after the Second World War and reminders of them are still common. Among our fruit trees an old horse plough lies rusting, and each year we say that we must save it and paint it. One farm in the village has a number of old rotting carts and waggons in the yard and we have an old horse's collar,

carthorse

with the stuffing coming out, that some hens have made into a nest. We even have a cart horse saddle, hanging on a wall, as well as several authentic horse brasses.

In my early childhood I remember being lifted onto the back of an old shire as it pulled a water cart to the cows in a meadow, and the movement and the sound of hooves on the metalled road remain surprisingly clear in memory. Now the sound of passing hooves still raises heads and many countrymen retain their interest in, and knowledge of horses. Most of the animals today are ridden by young girls or people who hunt, but whereas old villagers understand them, car drivers from the towns speed past with no knowledge and no care, as if a horse is a predictable machine. One evening proof of their independence was shown when a riderless skewbald pony galloped by, with saddle and bridle attached. It swerved past me easily, but a van driver stopped it on the old railway bridge, much to the relief of its rider, a young girl who had been thrown.

It was at this time too that I drove to a nearby town, for each year a shire-horse show is held for all those who remain interested in breeding, working and showing cart horses. Indeed a mixture of nostalgia and high oil prices have led to a revival in working horses and in the old ways.

The day was cold with a bitter north-west wind blowing, yet there was a large crowd. There were many elderly men present who had obviously worked with horses in earlier days on the land; they stood watching the great shires with the wind bringing water to their eyes, while a few, some with flat caps, still led their horses with affection and pride. Their faces were lined, showing the years and the hardness they had lived through, yet from the wrinkles around their eyes and the upward endings of their lips it was clear that laughter and contentment had also been with them. It was a time of mixed emotions, of happiness and of sorrow; there was the smell of horses, the creak of leather, the sound of harness, small ruts in the roadways where the waggons had passed, and there were the horses themselves with their ribbons, their plaited tails and manes, and their large yet careful hair-fringed hooves. It was a reminder of an earlier time, when nearly all the men of a village worked on the farms and before the internal combustion engine ruled the land, the roads, and the minds of the people. Yet the faces told of patience, satisfaction, and pride, virtues that the new age seldom praises, and the accents indicated that these feelings had once been almost universal.

In addition to the horses there were tents and stalls where books, food, and saddlery were sold, and those selling horse brasses and horse ornaments were packed with people. In the exhibition ring the highlight was a parade of horses with their waggons and carts. The carts were nearly all owned by breweries, not farms. An old man with a broad Norfolk accent understood the situation completely: 'All they've got to do is put 2p on a pint and they've soon got one of those.' As I drove away I couldn't help wondering what the next few years might bring. Would all the cows in the area soon be gone? And will they be remembered with the same affection as horses, by those who had to get up at six o'clock each morning to milk them?

At one time March was the month when frogs usually spawned in many parts of the parish; in ditches and dips, in ponds and puddles, and in numerous marshy places in low-lying meadows. With better drainage and effective farm sprays, their numbers have declined, causing the Common Frog, to become uncommon. Consequently most of the traditional spawning sites remain unvisited and some are actually dry.

Spawn is likely to appear at any time in March or April, and I have seen it early, with snow falling, and late, when it has almost been summer. Each spring I search for it, although I have not found any for two years. When it occurs in the brook it has to be taken out, for with the increased flow after rain, it gets washed away. I keep it in an aquarium until the tadpoles have developed their legs, and then the young frogs can be returned to the brook to fend for themselves. Even when spawn occurs in ponds it has to be hidden, to protect it from people with buckets and jam jars, who release the small frogs to die in gardens awash with weed-killer and insecticide, instead of back at their place of birth.

Throughout the month I searched, but there was little chance of finding any in the brook as the level was too high and the current too fast. None appeared in the nearby pond either; at one time it was the main breeding site for frogs in the area, but since the Water Authority lowered the water table the pond has usually been dry for most of the year, and the frogs have vanished with the water. Nobody hunts frogs or eats them, and so there is no pressure group to campaign for their welfare or to sing their praises; consequently the decline of the common frog has been slow and sure and nobody seems to be interested.

I visited the other ponds in the village too, in hope rather than certainty, but they had no frogs either, and showed little signs of life. One pond was dug out as a small reservoir several years ago, and in summer it can be attractive with swallows skimming over the water, dragonflies darting and dancing over their reflections, and water crowfoot floating its flowers around the edges. But on a miserable March day it seemed almost dead; it was cold and still, with no frogs, no spawn and no traces of tadpoles. The village pond was slightly better with a pair of mallards that had made it their home, but nothing more. At one time horses were watered there, farm cart wheels were washed in it and many newts bred beneath the surface. It has seen drama too; once it was pumped dry by a horse-drawn fire engine in an effort to put out the burning vicarage; on another occasion a depressed man committed suicide in it; during the Second World War some stolen ammunition was abandoned in its centre, and over the years generations of small boys have played around it, and fallen in to it. Children still sometimes enjoy it, but now most of its water runs off from the nearby road, which in winter contains much salt, the newt population has dwindled, and there are no frogs.

The old parish gravel pit also holds water and now forms a small blackwatered pond. Apart from a snipe probing with its long sensitive beak at the edge, it had nothing of interest, and I resigned myself to the fact that it would be another frogless year. Then, right at the end of the month I saw a boy on a bike with a jam jar full of spawn. He had found it in a ditch near the old gravel workings and was returning surplus spawn after putting some in his aquarium. The ditch had plenty of clear, clean, water and near a large mass of spawn two adult frogs floated close to one another as if they were about to mate. On seeing movement they dived; there were four altogether, with two more half hidden by water and overhanging ivy leaves. A path had been worn along the bank by school children on their half-term holidays, but they would soon be back at school, and if left alone, perhaps the frogs will be able to hang on in the ditch for a few more years.

During the late afternoon on a warm day I stood on the old railway bridge just watching and listening. A private road now runs underneath the arch, as the railway was removed several years ago, and its sides are covered with scrub. Robins were vigorously singing a territorial song, as were two hedgesparrows. Another 'hedgie-bet' then emerged and it became clear that there were two males and a female, with the cocks displaying, threatening, and waving their wings at each other, with occasional skirmishes. It was an interesting interlude of passion and posturing, and the general mood was shared further along the roadway as a fine cock pheasant pursued a rival. At this time of year there are always winners and losers, but in nature the losers seem to have no need for psychiatrists, mental welfare officers and sedatives, they get by. Indeed it also seems to be true that country people stand up to the stresses and strains of everyday life far better than those who have to live or work in the towns, and it is said that: 'Nature, time, and patience are the three great physicians.' Nature is a good teacher too, and there is much benefit in just watching the patterns of the wild.

As I watched however, it was obvious that few other people would learn from the activities beyond the bridge, for the commuters cars were carrying their occupants back to their implanted suburban homes in various villages. Many of the new commuters seem to have no time and little patience, and the ways of nature are not seen as they journey to and from their homes. Consequently both the birdsong and the springtime drama go by virtually unnoticed.

Because of this it is one of the unusual features of the age that although 'civilised' Western man claims to be intelligent and free, yet the average person is as conditioned as any sheep, ant or captive animal. Their behaviour is reminiscent of Pavlov's dogs and bound to various social and economic pressures. Each morning they drive past in a long line of traffic to the town, and each evening they return. They look pale, bored, tired and plugged in to a regular routine. They rarely seem to smile, and those with passengers appear to endure company in silence. Even at weekends their behaviour is often predictable with another journey into the town for shopping, and it is almost possible to check the time by some of them. They appear to lead colourless, routine lives and they get their excitement vicariously, seated in front of television sets.

The feathered commuters of winter and spring are far more interesting. Starlings fly to the farmyard every morning and afternoon, and I can watch them from my window as I work. They fly in a direct line, with occasional glides, in a similar way to seabirds as they fly to and from their nests. They come in ones and twos and perch in the weeping willow tree, waiting for Father or John to feed the cattle in the yard below, and then they glide down to feed. Some even fly into the sheds of the young calves to steal their meal and pellets, until they are full, or disturbed, and then they return to the tree where they sing their grating song and preen. Some are excellent mimmicks, and this year it has been the call of fieldfares that has been the one most often practised. If the morning drags, then they again glide down, to the lawn, where they walk about busily in search of 'leather jackets' and worms. They are attractive birds with a dark iridescent plumage that flashes with blue, violet and turquoise in bright light, but they are strange too, and as spring approaches they often sing their throaty song with their wings held open and their feathers ruffled. Then they look distinctly reptilian, an uncomfortable reminder of what the early ancestors of warm blooded life might have been.

In March the starlings are more welcome than usual, for they can indicate the true arrival of spring. To many country people the progression of the calendar is shown by a succession of natural events, the first violet, the finding of a wild rose, and the appearance of fieldfares. Spring can be shown by a number of firsts; the first cowslip, the first squashed hedgehog on the road, or the arrival of the cuckoo. To me however spring is shown by the change in the colour of the starlings beaks, for in winter they are as a dark as the soil in which they probe, but as the season changes, so does the colour, until each beak is a golden yellow. By the beginning of the month most had started to change, and by the end they were all bright and fresh. The human commuters, on the other hand, appeared to be just as drab as they were before.

April

❧

The infant april joins the spring
And views its watery skye
As youngling linnet tries its wing
And fears at first to flye

AWAY FROM THE WIND, the month started warm, with a
bright sun that seemed to make the singing of the birds
more vibrant. In a neighbour's garden pasque flowers were out, a
week late, for traditionally they flower by Easter Day, and the
name comes from the old French word for Easter, 'pasques'. It
was the combination of an early Easter and a cool spring that led
to the late flowering of this beautiful wild anemone. Unfortunately its beauty has been its greatest handicap, for now it is
rarely found growing in the wild, as people have picked it and
dug up whole plants, and so, in the main it is now confined to
private gardens.

While out one Sunday afternoon I saw a hare, the first I had
seen for several months. It had been crouching out of sight in its
form, but as I approached it left so quickly that it literally took
off, jumping into the air, with its ears erect. It looked absurd;
normally, when frightened or running at speed, the ears are held
flat, but this hare bounded along with its ears aloft. When I
looked into the form, a shallow depression scraped into the soil,
there were claw marks cut into the clay at the entrance, showing
the speed at which the hare had left. Several farmers have noticed
the fall in the number of hares in the parish over recent years, but
nobody seems to know the reason. The only explanation offered
stems from the old country belief that rabbits and hares don't

hare

mix, and because rabbits have become more plentiful, so hare numbers have fallen away.

The following week however, it seemed that there might be more hares about after all. The evidence came with a heavy fall of snow; it started as a flurry at midday and gradually settled into a steady fall with large flakes, that went on into the night. By morning it had stopped, but there had been a frost and three inches of snow carpeted the ground. It was fresh and crisp, with a clear blue sky. It was strange to see the daffodils with a coating of snow, and the garden primroses were completely covered. Warners Corner was still, and apart from the larks, quiet, but over its fifty acres the snow mapped out the activities of the night. Fox tracks criss-crossed the whole field, showing the presence of several, or the hunting habits of one; there were tracks of rabbits hopping around the burrows near the earth; the footprints and wing patterns of pheasants and partridges, and one track was unidentifiable, as if something had been dragged across the field, or possessed a large tail. But surprisingly hare tracks were numerous too, some went straight and some curved, and where several met, the snow was churned up in a small circle, showing that their March madness had gone on into April. Why I had not seen them, or the dogs disturbed them, on other days was a mystery and confirms the fact that the hare remains one of our most common but least known creatures.

During the day the snow thawed steadily and quickly, but it remained cold for over a week, and as the blackthorn came into blossom it gave its 'blackthorn winter'. The small white flowers

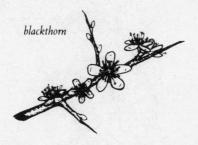

blackthorn

appeared before the leaves and it is a strange fact that the abundant blossom seldom produces a matching crop of sloes.

Gradually the land dried and those farmers with drilling to complete seemed to work all the hours of daylight. Spraying too was in progress and one tractor on the next farm became stuck up to its axles at the edge of a large field puddle. The usual cowslips flowered in the brook meadows, near the grassed relics of old gravel diggings, where weedkiller rarely blows. Each year they flower, and even with the cattle present it is surprising how few are grazed. At first glance along the base of the hedges the small hornlike flowers of ground ivy looked like violets, and by the brook, coltsfoot was already offering its seed-heads of white, weightless down, to the wind. It was while I was looking at some coltsfoot, close to where the small Tit Brook flows into the larger main brook, that the most memorable incident of the month occurred. I was thinking about the peculiarities of the plant; how the 'coltsfoot' shaped leaves rarely appear before the flowering cycle has finished, and how the flower stalk droops as the flower head dies, only to stand erect again when the seed-head ripens. Suddenly a shrill call came from Tit Brook and made me look up, beating wings and bright rufous breasts flashed by the bend into the main brook, and as they straightened up the kingfishers seemed to explode into streaks of vivid turquoise. They perched in some blackthorn on the opposite bank and one almost immediately dived into the gravelly shadows to emerge with a small fish. I was tense and still, for it seemed likely that I was about to see the courtship ritual in which the male turns the

kingfisher

fish in his bill to present it to his partner, head first, ready to swallow. It returned to its mate, but sadly my imagination was too far ahead of the actual action, for the four dogs blundered onto the scene, the birds flew off, and my chance was lost.

But among the stirrings of love and new life, there was also death. I saw my first hedgehog of the year flattened on the road, and surprisingly, a frog spreadeagled in the High Street; squashed no doubt as it went from garden pond to garden pond, looking for a mate. Suddenly, one evening, death also came to the farm. At first it seemed to be a normal calving, but after the front legs of the calf had emerged, the head would not come. John, Father, and Rachael all heaved and pulled together, while Robert, the Lakeland vet worked to ease the animal out. Briefly it kicked, as if desperate for lack of room, and when it eventually came, it was dead. Robert, with his arm exploring the inside of the cow informed us that she was badly ripped inside and would probably die, as there was nothing more he could do. Within an hour she was driven into a cattle truck for the 'knacker', who had agreed to stay open to take her. It was one of the best young cows in the herd and she would be shot prematurely for beef. As Rachael cleaned her boots, tears welled up into her eyes and Father was unusually quiet and looked tired. It was a small cow, supposedly 'in-calf' to a Friesian bull, yet the dead calf was a large beef Charolais; the glass tube of the inseminator had delivered the wrong goods, a mistake that a bull would not have made.

Along the road from the farm stands a pair of old cottages, and although one has been modernised, they both provide reminders of the old village. The only surviving parish pump stands outside one, and even during the great drought, cool clear water could be sent tumbling from its spout. In summer the backdoor is almost hidden by flowers; flowers from the traditional old rural garden and others that were once commonly found in the hedgerow and in the open field. For in addition to lavender, wallflowers and hollyhocks, it has comfrey, cowslips, primroses, pasque flowers and many more, together with a host of herbs and culinary plants that were once found in many country kitchens. The widow who lives there bought the cottage for a hundred pounds when she first moved into the village, and in it she has created a small refuge for country crafts, customs, and wayside flowers. She has old books, china, corn-dollies and friendship cushions that girls once made for their lovers, and she creates beauty from rags, dead flowers, and straw. She passes on her knowledge, as well as plants and seeds, to anybody who is interested, and through her, many of the old skills continue to survive.

Next door another widow lived, but she did not preserve the old ways, she actually lived them, for her life style varied little from the one she had lived as a young woman at the turn of the century. She had one cold water tap, and kept the day's supply stored in earthenware pots or jugs in the kitchen. She had an outside bucket lavatory and she cooked on an old kitchen range. The village had only been a quarter of its present size when she had moved in with her husband, who worked as a shepherd. Each day 'Crabby' had walked several miles to his sheep, and when shearers had been wanted in other villages he had visited them as well. In a tumble-down shed his crook, shears and sheep bells could still be seen, and at one time he had a large book of hand written remedies to cure all everyday ills.

Gradually the old lady became bent up and her sight dimmed, although she still tried to retain her independence and she refused to consider a new centrally-heated bungalow. She was the oldest inhabitant of the village and people were sorry when she died, although they were glad she had managed to miss the indignities of an old people's home. But even during sadness there was humour, for she had asked to be buried in the churchyard, next to her husband. The request was simple, but nobody could remember exactly where old Crabby had been buried, for he had professed to be 'chapel', and the vicar at that time had refused to record chapel burials. Messages were sent to the church wardens, the parish clerk, and several of the older villagers, to try to locate Crabby; a man who had been eccentric in life and now he continued his pleasure in death. Opinions were divided: 'He must be in there somewhere': 'We can't bury the old girl in any old spot', and 'Put her anywhere, it doesn't matter who you are next to down there.' Eventually somebody had a bright idea: 'Why not go and see Emily, she's bound to know, she goes to all the funerals.' Sure enough she had been to Crabby's, and knew, at least she thought she knew, which was his unmarked grave.

The ceremony was short and simple and the old lady went out in a grander style than she ever experienced while alive, for she was wheeled into the chapel on a stainless steel trolley, followed by the professional mourners who looked their part. The coffin stopped over the baptistry, making the wooden floor boards bend towards the water below, and then she was wheeled along Church Lane, across denominational boundaries, into the churchyard. The grave had been dug between two mounds, exposing one end of a neighbouring coffin. To Charlie this was no surprise: 'It's as overcrowded down there as it is up here; but at least it's quieter.'

Rooks have always been familiar birds in the parish, at all seasons of the year, but it is in the spring that their presence is most obvious as they caw and clamour in the rookery during all the hours of daylight. Nests are defended, sticks are stolen, eggs are incubated and the young are fed. Until a few years ago, two rookeries just over the parish boundary were used, but then, for no obvious reason, a few nests appeared in the spinney close to the farm. Now a thriving rookery has been established and one of the former sites is completely deserted, a situation which is supposed to bring misfortune to those living close by. We were pleased when the rooks arrived, for like many birds, they too have suffered as trees and hedgerows have been removed for the sake of agricultural efficiency, and although they are still common, their numbers have visibly declined.

Last year however, Dutch Elm Disease killed some of the trees which held the nests, and gales did the rest. By January only four dishevelled heaps of twigs remained, together with two ruins which would never hold eggs. To make matters worse the rooks seemed to have dispersed and rarely visited the spinney. Often they could be seen perching in the willows along the brook, as if they were considering another site. But then they returned: I heard them first on a bright windy morning early in the new year, when a noisy gang came flying low over the fields. They hedge-hopped the road and made straight for the rookery where they wheeled and perched and called, as if estimating the damage before another season began. After that they returned most days and gradually the pairing and repairing took place until there were again numerous nests among the tree tops.

Cawing and combat showed where territory was being defended and some fastidious birds seemed to prod, poke, dismantle and rebuild their piles of tangled twigs until the nests suited their exact requirements. From the outside it always seems remarkable that any eggs survive at all, but inside, the nests are lined with mud and straw, to bind, and to provide a softer surface.

By the beginning of the month twenty-four nests were occupied, and in grass fields and on newly sown corn the males fed their partners in courtship, with the wings of the wives held open like those of feeding young. Even in the treetops the displaying went on, with the males cawing and bowing to their brooding partners, between bouts of stealing from neighbours and flying off to feed. Rook eggs hatch after only a fortnight's incubation and the young fly after about a month; the rookery then quietens until the approach of the next season of building, fighting and breeding, when, according to tradition, each pair will return to their old nest site.

I spent several hours just watching the rooks about their business, and their calls have become part of the fabric of spring. At one time they were shot to prevent damage to corn, and an old country rhyme says: 'Four seeds you have to sow. One for the rook and one for the crow, one to die and one to grow.' Rook pie was also eaten, a dish that was said to be tasty and a way of preventing hair from turning grey.

Rooks can damage crops, but they can also do much good, as they eat many wireworms and leather-jackets. Indeed as they fly in on their ragged edged wings and then walk slowly about or hop from furrow to furrow, they look pompous and superior. With their thick thigh feathers they have the appearance of country gentlemen wearing fashionably cut plus-fours. Often, in wind, they seem to fly for the sheer enjoyment of tossing and tumbling in moving air, and it is possible to make weather predictions from their behaviour. They also seem to have a well developed communal life and social order, and because of the way in which they sit around in rookeries, there are stories of meetings, parliaments, rook courts and even evictions.

I hope that the rooks remain in the spinney, despite Dutch Elm Disease, for rooks are a part of the English country landscape, and a rookless spring would seem empty and almost ominous. But the warnings are present and if the mixture of disease and destruction continues to denude the parish of trees, then the rook could become a bird simply of distant memory and ancient country lore.

Rooks were not the only ones to hold court during the month, for one Tuesday evening the Annual Parish Meeting was held in the Village Hall. It is an interesting event, for it gives all parishioners the chance to criticise or to praise the way in which village affairs have been handled over the preceding twelve months. As a forum it is unique, providing an opportunity quite unknown to those who live in towns and cities.

By the time the chairman began the meeting, twenty-two people were present, eighteen more than the year before, so an evening of varying entertainment was assured. The first part of the proceedings was formal with reports and statements by various representatives and councillors. It was revealed that only fifty-nine children attended the village school, including sixteen from other villages, the lowest figure for many years. Consequently it was suggested that if the Education Authority should happen to awake from its slumbers, it might try for closure, as an economy measure, despite the fact that village schools, large and small, contribute to village life. Serious warnings were then given by the County Councillor of the 'grave dangers' that could result from the population getting out of balance, and already, he said, there were more old people than young, and in the future the situation could become alarming, with comparatively few young people and a vast army of elderly and infirm all needing care.

After an hour all the business had been completed except the one item that everyone really wanted: 'Any Other Business'. Normally that is a time of chaotic debate, about such weighty matters as the village pond, the recreation ground, or even lamp posts, and once a subject has been mentioned, then complaints and fears multiply until it seems remarkable that ordinary people have managed to survive at all in the face of such enormous difficulties. In past years the pond has been typical, for whenever it has been mentioned it has ceased to be a small area of water for newts and the occasional duck, but it has become an eye-sore, a health hazard, a danger to children, and a potential disaster area for all road transport. Similarly the recreation ground has been seen as a dog latrine, a harbour for hooligans, and a place where all manner of wicked and shameful pastimes are practised.

With such a tradition to carry on, it came as a surprise when silence followed the announcement of 'Any Other Business'; it was as if those present were struggling to find something different. It was a small elderly bespectacled lady who spoke first: 'When is the Church Lane going to be cleaned?' she asked innocently; so this year it was going to be something new, Church Lane, a small path between the church and the vicarage, which also passes two small cottages and the chapel.

It was a popular choice, for immediately someone else chimed in: 'Oh yes, it's a disgrace. All those weeds make your legs wet, I don't suppose they'll be cut down because some people like them.' It was explained that since the village roadmen, with their brooms and wheelbarrows had been 'phased out', a gang of motorised roadsweepers was supposed to visit the village every six weeks, and they would be told.

'And another thing', came the voice of a chapel goer, 'what about all those overhanging branches hitting the chapel roof, they could knock the slates off and kill somebody?'

'What trees? Where are they? What are you talking about?' asked another.

'They're in the vicarage, they should be lopped off before they do any damage.'

It seemed that a church/chapel confrontation was inevitable, until a new voice added:

'And that's not all, somebody's been riding a motorbike up there too.'

The chapel lady could beat that easily: 'Why that's nothing, it's used by horses. They could trample you to death. What do they want to use it for?'

'Perhaps they're going to church.' someone muttered.

'It's not horse property, they should get off before they knock us off. We need a gate at each end before somebody gets injured.'

'If there were gates at each end you could walk into them in the dark and break your legs.'

'Why not graze horses in the churchyard?'

'Why not keep them off our footpath?'

The argument ebbed and flowed, and like the pond before, Church Lane became a place of great danger and potential threat. After every aspect of its iniquities had been explored, all seemed satisfied and it was agreed that the horses should be kept away, the weeds should be cut and the trees should be lopped. The village meeting had again been a success, those with ears to hear had heard, those with grievances to air had complained, and all those present had been well entertained.

At the other end of the village a resident had taken the law into his own hands to stop horses, especially those walking over the grass verge in front of his house. He had erected two notices proclaiming: 'No horses'; underneath, a different hand had added: 'Indians Dismount'.

During the warm weather in the early part of the month, the fields began to dry and the grass freshened to begin its summer growth. Fertiliser was spread on it too, for contrary to the normal town view, grass is not 'free' and it has to be carefully looked after. Each winter the cows are kept in a yard away from the cold wet land, but as the days lengthen and the grass grows, they seem to know that soon they will again be released to the comparative freedom and comfort of grazing in the fields. It was on a bright Thursday morning that the yard gate was opened; they needed no second invitation, they twitched their ears, frisked their tails, and the younger animals galloped along the roadway to the meadow. The older matrons were just as eager and trotted briskly behind with their pendulous udders swinging freely from side to side. Once in the field they galloped, pranced and bucked in sheer enjoyment and anticipation, and each year we make a point of watching their celebration. Some ran with their tails held upright, as they do when the gad flies bite later in the summer, some kicked out in unrestricted pleasure, and some jousted in mock, hornless battle.

Once grass is eaten, so the milk yield increases and the colour changes until the cream is a light yellow. The smell of the milk can change too, and if the pasture is rich in clover it can smell and taste sweet, while in the past when meadows were infested with wild 'crow onions', the milk took the flavour of the weeds. At milking time the milk is sucked into a large refrigerated tank, and each morning it is collected by tanker lorry. We drink the milk unpasteurised, as it comes out of the cows, which means that we can enjoy real butter, cream and cheese.

The butter too changes colour in the spring, from white to rich yellow. The cream is poured into a small glass churn with wooden paddles and stirred vigorously. It gradually thickens until suddenly coagulation takes place as the butter separates from the buttermilk. It is then drained and washed with cold water to swill out the remaining liquid. Half a teaspoonful of salt is added to each pound of butter and, in the absence of proper butter pats, it is patted with wet wooden spoons to squeeze it drier, and then it is ready to eat.

We eat milk cheese too, which is an old country food made from sour milk. The milk is left in a bowl in the warm kitchen until it turns sour, which in warm thundery weather may be only a few hours. It is then tipped into a muslin cloth, which is tied at the top to make a bag, and left to drain, either hanging up, or in a colander. When it ceases to drip it is ready to be eaten. It is white, soft and crumbly, and can be added to a salad, like ordinary cheese, or it can be eaten with salt, pepper, vinegar, and slices of bread and butter.

Occasionally we even make clotted cream, for that too can be made from fresh milk. The milk has to be taken warm, as it comes from the cows, and left to stand over-night, to allow the cream to rise. It is then heated very slowly to just under boiling point, and the 'clotted cream' is scooped from the surface. When it is cool it makes a pleasant luxury and is just as good as the famous cream made in Devon and Cornwall.

The other main food we get from cows is 'bisning custard', made from thick 'bisnings' that come from a cow immediately it has calved. It is thick and yellow, and as it contains various anti-bodies it is vital to the calf to give protection against disease. When sugar is added and it is heated in the oven, it sets like an egg custard, but has much more flavour. It can be eaten by itself or used instead of ordinary custard.

Regrettably, fresh untreated milk is becoming harder to buy, and some people even refuse to drink it. We are lucky however and fresh milk, butter, cheese, cream and bisnings will continue to form part of our uncivilised and unprocessed diet, even if, officially, they are considered to be 'a hazard to health'.

May

❧

Come queen of months in company
Wi all thy merry minstrelsy
The restless cuckoo absent long
And twittering swallows chimney song

MAY IS USUALLY my favourite month, for it is a time of full
blossom, birdsong, young life and regeneration. Although
I saw my first swallow on the last day of April, and more followed soon after, it was a cold wet start to the month. It is said
that warm weather never sets in until the 'paigles' (cowslips) are
finished, and so it proved to be. Early one morning a cuckoo sang;
its song was brief and I did not hear it from the farm again. Just a
few years ago the sound of cuckoos calling could be heard during
all the days of May, but now they seem to move quickly on, to
areas where food and cover are more plentiful.

John finished cultivating the last arable field, and despite the
warning of low yields from barley sown after the arrival of the
cuckoo, he decided to plant some 'cuckoo barley'. The best guide
for sowing spring barley comes from the elm, for 'When the elm
leaf is as big as a mouse's ear, then sow thy barley never fear.'
With the drill hitched up to the tractor and the seed corn loaded
onto the trailer, it started to rain. It rained all day, and the water
level of the ditch alongside the farm rose steadily and threatened
to flood. The concrete pipes under a nearby front garden had
become blocked with debris, and Father could not clear them
with his drain rods. Because of the urgency he cut the bottom out
of a plastic bucket to fix to the rods, to make a plunger, which he
pushed and pulled up the pipes. 'It's worked', he said, with wish-
ful thinking, as the slow trickle continued. He tried again; it

57

worked the second time and a great surge of water almost filled his wellington boots.

His efforts were in vain for the rain continued throughout the night and in the morning the ditch had overflowed. The cars were flooded in the garage, all that could be seen of the lawnmowers were their handles, in the yard, calves were splashing about up to their hocks, and the daffodils that had been bent over with snow, were now surrounded by water. The rain had been aided by workmen at the sewage pumping station across the road, who, to ease the burden of their pumps had used lorries with additional pumps to get the water and sewage out, oblivious to the fact that it was flowing straight over the road and into the farmyard, which is slightly lower.

The brook flooded in a way that it had not done for years. The willows were again isolated islands in brown swirling water and the level was so high that where the water narrowed to pass under the road, there was no gap between the top of the bridge and the gushing torrent. If there is any truth in the old saying 'a wet May, brings a good load of hay', then the hay crop will be exceptional.

By the next afternoon the floods had subsided. Dead reeds fringed the meadow fences, some of which had been smashed by floating logs and branches. Surprisingly lesser celandines and Jack-by-the-hedge were already flowering, with their bright petals showing up vividly against the silt stained leaves.

Warm weather came, but the land was still much too wet to work. Wallflowers and lilac gave their summer scents to the garden and the fields of rape formed blocks of brilliant mustard yellow. Some flowering rape could be seen in the roadside verges, showing how spilled and blown seed has helped to turn it into a common wayside flower. Bumble and honey bees flew to the flowering fields, but one afternoon, after a farmer had sprayed his wheat across their flight path, they died before they could reach their source of food. It is interesting how field colours show the changing fashions of farming; at one time there were lakes of deep sea blue where fields of linseed grew; then came pink pools of sanfoin, and now they have given way to a patchwork quilt of corn and oilseed rape. The rape is grown for the rich protein content of its seed, which is used in cattlefeed and in margarine.

The 'cuckoo barley' was eventually sown despite the drill becoming bogged down on several occasions, and the month settled back to normality. The cow parsley, waist high and white, fringed the garden and the roadside verges, living up to its country name of Queen Anne's lace. In a boggy ditch the large marsh marigold that a neighbour had rescued from the brook, before the mechanical draglines could rip it out, was a mass of bright yellow flowers, and the red buds of apple blossom burst into fading pink cups of gentle fragrance and fragile beauty. Yellow rocket and buttercups joined the flowers of the jungle and brook banks, and in shady places in gardens and hedgerows the cuckoo pint flowered. It is a strange plant; a large cape-like leaf unfurls

cuckoo pint

revealing a brownish stem, below which and out of sight are a number of small flowers. The buds of the spinney elms gradually burst into leaf, giving an iridescent green haze to the lucid shafts of sunlight. The boughs of 'may' became heavy with blossom and the hot sun gave patches of light and moving shade to the fresh green canopy of the garden silver birches. The light green of the lime leaves had the luminous gloss and texture of early summer and new oak leaves appeared with the leafless ash still only showing its feathery flowers. After all the rain it was a promising sign, for: 'If the oak is out before the ash, then you'll only get a splash.'

On a hot afternoon in the 'jungle' I looked up when I heard a wren sing and caught a glimpse of a tree-creeper, feeding and searching busily in the cracks and crevices of a willow trunk. It matched the bark perfectly with the lightness of its breast and the darkness of its back complimenting the contrasts of light and shade. Further along, as the dogs went after a rabbit, a hedge-sparrow flew in alarm from a small compact hawthorn bush. Hidden within was a' small nest lined with moss and cow-hair, containing four perfectly matched eggs of clear sky-blue. A female mallard and seven small ducklings were swimming on the brook, but on seeing the dogs and me, the young paddled noisily into the bankside weeds. The mother, sitting low in the water, splashed her wings feigning injury, making the dogs run off in excited pursuit. She led them well over fifty yards downstream before calmly taking off and flying in a wide half circle back to her brood. There is usually a nest along the willows every year; in most instances the young hatch several feet up and then tumble down to the ground. The way in which the mother imitates injury is convincing and fascinating, but it poses unanswerable questions: is it an instinctive response? Does the bird learn the reaction from observing its own mother? Or does it decide on the display using its own intelligence?

At one time many of the local parishes celebrated May Day, the first day of the month, but the form of the festivities varied from village to village. The origin of the day goes back many centuries to pre-Christian times when it was a celebration of new growth and fertility, but gradually it developed simply into a day when the approach of summer could be anticipated. In Tudor times it was a public holiday, when all classes were up at dawn to go 'a-maying'; then the revelries lasted well into the night and were frowned upon by the puritans. One of them described maypoles as those 'stinkyng idols', and complained that they made the people 'leape and dance, as the heathen did'. Cromwell did not approve of the cavorting, and in 1644 maypoles were banned, a prohibition which continued until the arrival of Charles II.

Following the Restoration many of the traditions continued into this century and there are still old village people who remember May Day as one of the highlights of each school year. In fact it was often only bettered by Empire Day, when school children actually saluted the flag, and were taught the wonders of *Pax Britannica*.

Many of the May Day celebrations involved the use of flowers, and the flowering hawthorn, which featured in crowns and garlands, was known as 'may', although now it is seldom out on the first of the month. This is simply because old May Day fell on

flowering 'may'

13th May, when the 'may' was beginning to flower. The calendar was changed in 1752, when Britain was several days behind the rest of Europe, and so the Gregorian Calendar was adopted, for uniformity. Consequently the day after May Day became the fourteenth, and riots followed, involving all those who thought that they were being cheated out of a fortnight.

In the old days the activities of May Day started before dawn with 'May-Birching', when sprigs or branches were put on cottage doorsteps to show how neighbours viewed the occupants. To get hawthorn, lime, apple, or pear, was good, brambles or blackthorn was bad, whereas if a woman found elder, it meant that her morals left something to be desired. Many people went out at dawn to kiss the dew, which was said to bring them luck. While if young girls washed themselves with May Day morning dew, it was thought to make them more beautiful, and many even believed that it would improve their complexions and take away freckles.

Once the sun was up, customs varied from parish to parish. In one village girls would adorn themselves with daisy chains and poses, and skip around the village, while in the next, cowslips might be the chosen flower for garlands, crowns and cowslip-balls. Multi-coloured garlands were popular in many places and coloured ribbons were used together with primroses, daisies, buttercups, wallflowers and apple and pear blossom. After the flowers had been picked, then houses could be visited, as it was the custom for the residents to be greeted with song in return for a penny. In a neighbouring village they sang:

> On bright May day,
> With garlands gay,
> We march along the street.
> With many a crown and wreath beneath,
> The Maypole we shall greet.

Often the journey to the maypole was made in procession, with the prettiest girl, the May Queen, leading with her attendants.

Over the years the celebrations for May Day have gradually died. When in short trousers in the infant room of the village school I went with the rest of the children to another school to watch their maypole dancing, and briefly, like all the other little boys, I fell in love with the May Queen, with her flowers, her long white dress and her dancing eyes. Now few people celebrate May Day; it did not really matter this year, for the day was cold and wet and most people simply spent the holiday in front of their television sets, as usual.

With the fine weather I moved Rusty out to her summer run. It was over-grown with grass and cow-parsley, but it gives her freedom to play, sleep, dig holes, and catch the unwary bird or animal that wanders through the wire. May is also another of the months when wild foxes can be seen, especially if the cubs are occupied in play around the entrances of their earth. The grass and corn has not grown to its full concealing summer height, and cub watching can be a tense and rewarding pleasure. I still did not know whether the Warners Corner earth was occupied, but I knew that cubs had already been born elsewhere, for a woman from the next village had telephoned me about a cub that she had found wandering at the side of the road. It was small, with its eyes just open, probably no more than a fortnight old. Its coat

fox cub

was soft and downy and when handled it cried faintly. It was slightly emaciated too, but gradually it was learning to drink milk from a saucer. Close to where it was found some trees had been cut down and it is likely that because of the disturbance the vixen had intended to move her family to a safer, quieter place. In the middle of the operation she had probably been frightened by the approach of a car or a person, and dropped the cub. If it had then been placed in one of the adjoining fields, the vixen would have searched for it, but instead the cub had a new home and a new foster mother.

I decided that the only way to find out if cubs were present at Warners Corner was to sit outside the earth. The previous year, a vigil outside an earth at the rifle range had been well worthwhile for no fewer than six half grown cubs had emerged and proceeded to play some thirty yards away. They had fought, stalked, pounced, jumped, and rolled together in the natural play of young hunters, until suddenly they had stopped. They had looked eastwards before bounding off down the gentle hill towards the middle of a field. From the greetings whimpers and whines, similar to the ones Rusty makes to me, I had assumed that they were meeting the vixen who was returning with food. I had then moved to try to get a better view, but the old fox must have seen me for she had screamed in warning and the cubs had scampered back to the holes and disappeared underground.

The evening I chose to watch the earth was cloudy but warm, with about an hour and a half to sunset. I approached along one of the brook meadows and then stood in a hedge about forty yards away from the holes at the base of a hawthorn hedge. There were no signs of foxes and all was quiet except for the birds and the drone of distant tractors working until the last of the light. Yellowhammers and larks were singing and suddenly the warning cry of a blackbird rattled out. What caused its alarm I could not see and I wished that I possessed the knowledge of some old gamekeepers who claim to be able to tell what disturbs blackbirds by the tone and the intensity of their alarm signal. The grating calls of partridges carried from beyond the brook and a cock pheasant strolled over close to the earth. It stood erect and called, flapping its wings as it did so, rather like a cockerel crowing; no rival replied and so it walked through the hedge and out of view.

Close to the earth a rabbit with her three young ones were out feeding; they had grown since the day when I had first seen them in March. Occasionally they would run and jump in play, their white 'cotton-tails' showing up clearly in the fading light. A rustle betrayed a rabbit leaving the hedge a few yards away from me; it was so close that I could actually hear it nibbling grass. After biting off several stalks it would sit up with four or five long pieces of grass hanging from its mouth; then, without using its front paws, it would chew quickly and the grass would be drawn up into its mouth until it disappeared, almost as if it was saying 'look, no hands'. From time to time it would sit up, working its ears in all directions for danger and looking straight at me, yet it was not alarmed, showing that stillness can be a most effective and simple camouflage. Eventually it moved off and I decided to measure the distance it had been from me – a mere eight paces. Eight yards out into the field I looked up, and there, thirty yards away, sitting looking at me through the long grass, was a full grown fox. Its ears were upright and its eyes were full of enquiry. We studied each other for several seconds, before it quietly turned and vanished into the hedge without any sign of panic. I had seen no cubs but I felt satisfied with an evening well spent.

The first Tuesday in May is the day of the Over Sixties Party, when all the members of the Over Sixties Club, and their guests, meet for food, fellowship and entertainment in the Village Hall. Some of the fellowship is qualified of course: 'Oh, I thought he would be here, he only comes when there's a free feed', but on the whole they all seem to get on well. There was salad, trifle and cream cakes supplied by a friendly extrovert baker who lives in the village. A special iced birthday cake also looked good; it was cut by a remarkable old lady who had made the cake for the previous twenty-seven years, but she had finally decided to give the honour to somebody else. After the food the tables were put away for the evening's entertainment; a visit from the Salvation Army. Most there expected members of a band and a session of singing old songs and hymns. Instead they were confronted by electric guitars, a set of drums and the more traditional tambourines.

Although the Over Sixties Club provides many retired people with companionship and an outside interest, some people refuse to join, for they do not consider themselves to be really old. One retired farmworker who lives in the High Street is scornful: 'Why should I go up there for tea and biscuits when I can have tea and biscuits at home. In any case I haven't got time to play silly games and listen to the women talking behind their hands – "Have you heard about Mrs. so-and-so", and "do you know what Mrs. somebody else is doing?", it's bloody silly. And then there are the outings to the sea. You get there and look at the sea, and then you walk along the beach and look at the sea, and then you have dinner looking at the sea, and then you look in a few shop windows, and then for a change you look at the sea.'

He is an amusing old cynic and he keeps the world right as he leans on his garden gate or takes his dog for a walk. I saw him one afternoon as he was gardening: 'Look at that garden over there', he said, pointing to a neighbour's overgrown garden, 'he lost his lawnmower in there last week and now he's trying to get a gun so that he can have a day's shooting in it. When I was a young man we had to work hard; seven or eight of us would scythe and clear a ten-acre field in a day. At harvest time we would start at four in the morning, stopping for sevensies, ninesies, elevensies, dinner and foursies, and we would have a pint of beer at each stop. We drank home-brewed beer and took it to the fields in homemade casks. It was better than the gassy stuff they call beer today. Considering the way they behave now when they've got this weak old stuff in them, if they drank the old beer then the only building we would want in the village would be an asylum, and if punk rockers had it you would need a machine gun to control them. The food was better in the old days too, more wholesome. We had turnips, swedes and even crab apples, but today its all artificial and gas. Even through the winter the children went to school in short trousers and sometimes they were so cold that they had to jump up and down in class to keep warm, yet they were fitter then than they are now. You don't even have to work on the dole today. I was unemployed in 1931 after working on a farm when the price of wheat went down to 18s 6d a quarter* and I had to go to the relieving officer for hand-outs. I was one of forty unemployed and was given one pound a week. I had to report to the workhouse in the next village between nine and five, sifting sand. We would sift the same heap three or four times a week. Later the unemployed were given ditches to clean out. They should give 'em something to do now. Today you only have to say you're off your rocker and spend a couple of days in a lunatic asylum and you can stay at home and get more money than those at work.

---

*A quarter was two combs or coombs. A comb of wheat weighs eighteen stone.

What a way to carry on. I know a man now who's sick. I've never seen him cutting the hedge with the handles of his hedge clippers, yet they say he's off his rockers. Like the bloke in the mental hospital who used to go about all day with a wheelbarrow turned upside down. "It isn't the wrong way round", he'd say, "if it was the other way up people would put things in it." But you don't want to hear about the past and present, you want to hear about the future. Well that's simple – if we keep going on as we are we will be buggered.'

The old farmworker is right, he has no need of the Over Sixties Club. The village has need of him however, for half an hour spent talking to him can throw new light on problems as diverse as politics, technological progress, curing warts with sloes, and the best ways of looking after carthorses.

Cuckoos and swallows were not the only summer visitors to arrive during the month, for early on, accompanied by the sound of hooves and turning cartwheels, gypsy Jim moved into the village. Each winter he pitches camp in a small field two miles along the road, with his horse-drawn gypsy caravan, a cart, an ordinary caravan, a portable shed, his wife and various children. Then within six months he migrates to the drift for the summer; he makes the trip to avoid paying rates, so it is said. This year however, he did not really want to move because of the mess left by the didecoys, but as he had nowhere else to go, the drift again became his home.

At one time he travelled the whole year round, wheeling and dealing, and the name Loveridge shows his genuine gypsy descent. He would buy and sell horses, make pegs, do seasonal farm-work, and sharpen scissors, knives and lawnmowers. But with the increasing volume of cars and lorries taking the attraction away from the open road, and because of friendships he made in the area, he dropped his traditional wandering and now he travels just four miles a year; two miles each way in the early summer and late autumn. His greeting of; 'Hallo guvner, are you alright?' is genuine, and he still rides around the villages sharpening scissors; when he gets custom he lifts his bike up on to its stand and pedals hard to work his belt driven grind-stone. He retains his skill of peg making in the old way, using willow that has been stripped of its bark and left to dry for a day in the wind. It is then cut into lengths and split, and the split of each peg is controlled by a thin metal strip that is cut from an empty tin can. There is now no demand for gypsy made pegs and when his wife knocks on cottage doors with her basket selling lace, needles and cotton, her pegs are cheap and mass produced. Occasionally the horse is used to make expeditions to collect scrap, old bikes and mowers, but most of the summer it lives a life of idleness, tethered along the grass verge.

Jim is at his best in the pub where the angle of his cap shows the amount of his alcoholic intake, and once the peak is over his left ear, it means that he is ready for home. Several times he has been found crawling in the middle of the road, and it is not unknown for him to cycle into a hedge. His gypsy remedy for drunkenness is simple: 'If you are a good sociable man and you are drunk, go home and have a long sleep.' He never gets aggressive when drunk, and to him the world seems to get a better place with every pint. As he talks he will offer to buy or sell anything that takes his fancy. He will offer money for gold watches or old junk, he will arrange to sell hens or even his dog if he thinks the price is right, and one evening he offered me his fine gypsy caravan, a 'vardo', for five hundred pounds.

His camp site smells of smoke and his life is still that of a gypsy, albeit an almost stationary one. He claims to be a Romany, and that he can talk their language with his sons, and when he is ill he uses the traditional gypsy remedies. The treatment varies from the use of honey for boils, to 'cowshit' for bald-headed women.* He says that his sister was once bald until cowpats were used, and now she's got the best head of hair you've ever seen.' One of his most reliable cures involves the use of ground ivy, which can be boiled in lard and used to cure eczema, while if ground ivy is boiled in water it can be used as an eye wash for men or dogs. His strangest remedy involves the use of 'Robin's Pillows', the moss-like wild rose galls containing wasp larvae, for when boiled in sugar they are said to ease whooping cough. He even recom-

---

*See *Cures and Remedies: The Country Way*.

mends hedgehog oil for earache, but unlike some gypsies who bake their hedgehog encased in clay, he insists that the hedgehog should be shaved of its bristles and roasted on a spit.

His knowledge of medicine extends to the animals he uses, particularly the horse: 'If they can't pee you give them old beer and vinegar, and to make their coats shine you give them plenty of carrots. To make a cock fight you let it run with the hens beforehand. You can't give them anything to stop them chasing hens, if you could my wife would make me have some as she says that I should know better at my age.'

When Jim goes, no doubt his horse and caravan will disappear too, as already his sons use vans and trucks. Despite calling people 'boss', or 'guvner', he is nobody's servant and he is proud of his independence. Although he is likeable and friendly, he is no saint and whenever he does a deal he will make sure that he is not the loser, even if he has to bend the rules. His philosophy is summed up by the way he deals in horses: 'You make a three year old horse a four year old by knocking some of its teeth out with a bit of metal like a chisel. It's not cheating really, 'cause it will be four next year so no harm's done.'

June

Now summer is in flower and natures hum
Is never silent round her sultry bloom
Insects as small as dust are never done
Wi' glittering dance and reeling in the sun

T HE MONTH STARTED CLEAR and hot, with open skies and a shimmering heat. The grasses along the brook meadows flowered, and walking through them sent small shifting clouds of pollen drifting on the breeze. When John cut them for hay, the fragrance hung in the air until after the rows had been turned ready for baling. The process of hay making is far faster than in the days of rakes and pitch-forks, but the words of Thomas Hood still hold good:

> *Oh! there's nothing in life like making love,*
> *Save making hay in fine weather.*

The flowers of May seemed to melt with the heat and the leaves of the trees became a deeper green. Elder flowers replaced those of the whitethorn in the hedges, like sheltered patches of lingering snow, and hogweed ousted the finer florets of Queen Anne's Lace. Adult rooks were joined by their young in the fields, and on the bank of one of the brookside cattle drinking places, a pair of partridges ruffled their feathers and bathed in the dust. Skylarks sang high above the fields and turtle doves murmured in the hedges, with the sun catching their rich chestnut wings and the white edging of their tails, when they flew. In the garden a bright male chaffinch sang his song, as his partner sat tight on her nest, and orange-tip butterflies flitted over the flower beds. The duck-

70

lings were still on the brook, but they had learnt, for when the dogs approached they quietly swam with their mother to the far bank and skulked in the nettles; the dogs did not see them, and there was no need for display.

The hay was baled in the heat; it is a dusty, noisy job, and Foss will not go into a field where a baler is working, for the rhythmic pounding of the machine sounds too much like thunder or shots from a gun. Tinker however, desperately wanted the freedom of the fields, for she was on heat and kept under tight control. Due to her age, her last litter had nearly killed her, she had struggled for breath and the task of producing milk had made her stagger, requiring a visit from the vet; but instinct was stronger than memory, and several times she tried to make off. She is fussy about who receives her favours; one hopeful suitor she attacks with her hackles up, but to find her 'husband', a black dog even older than her, Tinker will trek to the next village. Eventually, with just a few days of confinement to go, she slunk off after a long walk. She returned five hours later with her ears back and her tail wagging, with the grey muzzled 'husband' loitering behind. The next day she was taken to the vet to undo the work that had been done, with an injection. It meant that her passion had to last for another three weeks, but it was worth it for puppies were avoided. Robert, the vet, also had some good news, for the lumps around Tinker's nipples had not grown; he had some bad news too, for old bitches do not have a menopause.

At the start of the second week the radio announced a period of fine weather, which would enable us to get the hay home and the grass of Horse Field cut. Despite that it clouded over, and on the fourteenth, after drizzle, it rained. It was more than the ending of the hot spell, it was an ominous sign, for the fourteenth is St Vitus's Day:

> *If St Vitus Day be rainy weather,*
> *It will rain for thirty days together.*

As the rain came down I hurried to the meadows to stand the bales against each other, to prevent them from becoming sodden. They were heavy, damp, and awkward, and soon I was soaked to the skin. Showers followed on most days, and between them, when they were considered to be dry enough, the bales were loaded onto a trailer and carted back to the farm. On one journey father managed to turn the trailer over, which was no mean feat, for the field is flat; fortunately no harm was done as Charlie's hobble prevented him from riding on the load. The trailer was soon righted and gradually a section of the Dutch barn was filled; it is good to see, for it means that there will be a ready supply of fodder during the winter. Bale-cart is heavy work, pitching bales onto the trailer and then humping them into the barn, and it is made harder by the fact that hay bales are not a regular size or weight like straw.

On a number of mornings the old maxim of:

> *Rain before seven,*
> *Fine before eleven*

was shown to be accurate and there were several hot humid days. On one, I saw a kestrel wheeling and hovering high above. At times it seemed little more than a small moving speck, higher than I had ever seen one before, as if carried by a thermal on its open wings. Field beans came on flower, giving their sweet scent to the humid atmosphere, and the winter wheat and barley came

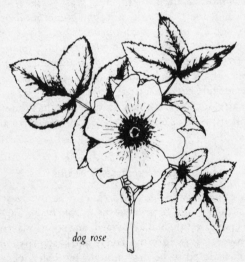

dog rose

out on ear. It is said that 'harvest is six weeks from earing to shearing', a saying that dates from the time when the corn was 'sheared' with scythes. Dog roses too came out with their beautiful but simple blooms, another indication of the short time to harvest. By a bridge of old railway sleepers, over Tit brook, the roses climbed to a height of fifteen feet and together with brambles, they looked like jungle creepers, trailing over two hawthorn trees. One afternoon, under the dark dome of interwoven canopies, a family of wrens was picking insects from the leaves, and occasionally a parent would feed one of its less successful young. While on a bright, sunny morning, two half grown lapwing chicks, looking fluffy and ungainly, walked at the side of the road, as their parents flew and cried out in alarm, trying to coax them onto safer ground.

When a fine forecast eventually came, John cut the remaining grass for hay; a hen pheasant flew, just before the knife, losing some of her feathers, and John took her eight eggs to put under a broody hen. The forecast again proved to be totally wrong, and he should have remembered the old saying: 'Three fine days and a thunder storm.' A great spiral of deep black cloud curled over the farm, rain and thunder came with it, and Foss jumped frantically at the door latch to let herself into the house. Rain returned on most days, and right at the end of the month a heifer got into a neighbour's wheat, after a storm. Water lodged heavily in the ears and I got soaked once more as I waded through the crop to drive her back over the brook.

Although harvesting the hay proved difficult, one harvest was completed easily, for I collected a basket full of elderflowers for winemaking. Elder grows in most hedgerows, and although many people treat it as a 'weed', it is a pleasant plant. Sometimes it grows as a bush, with numerous stalks shooting up from the ground, and others develop into small trees. Birds are the greatest spreaders of elder, dropping the ripe berries and passing out the seeds over a wide area once the fruit has been eaten. Even where rabbits are present elder grows well, for it is one of the few trees they dislike. It is a useful plant, the pithy centres of the young stems can be hollowed out to make pea-shooters or musical-pipes, the old wood is hard and good for burning when dry, and is used for making spoons. Even the leaves have a function and old horsekeepers would fix them to the bridles of their horses to keep the flies away.

An elder bush grows up every spring in front of Rusty's summer run, and each year I cut it down and use the shoots as markers for the rows of vegetables in the garden. Sometimes the larger cuttings take root, and despite its rough treatment, every year the bush grows again.

I picked the elderflowers from a high overgrown hedge that borders the small orchard, which runs as an extension to the kitchen garden. The large white flowerheads are made up of numerous clusters of small florets, each one being a miniature flower in its own right, with five white petals. The smell is musky, but not unpleasant, and as each cluster is picked, yellow pollen and white petals shower down. I was not the only one interested in the elder flowers, for the bushes were alive with insects, spiders and moths. Some spiders had round lime-green bodies, and when an attractive moth flew and settled with its wings open, it looked exactly like a dead leaf (a yellow shell moth). On being disturbed a small white moth also flew for cover, it had ragged wings that had the strange appearance of feathers. Picking elderflowers is a peaceful and relaxing exercise, and can be recommended.

The actual wine is easy to make; the florets are shredded from the main stalks with a fork, and a quart is then tipped into a plastic bucket, so that one and a half gallons of boiling water can be poured over them, and the mixture should then be well stirred. When visitors call they ought to be told that elderflower wine is being made, for the process makes the whole house smell like tom-cats. After ten days the liquid should be strained off through muslin so that three pounds of sugar and an ounce of yeast can be added; it should then be left in a large fermentation jar until it stops fermenting. This simple method can be used for all types of country wine and it is usually successful. It is much less trouble than measuring exact quantities and using special yeasts, like some enthusiastic winemakers, for they tend to take the enjoyment out of production and the surprise out of the end result.

Part of the pleasure of making elderflower wine is derived

from the fact that before the process can start, the fermentation jars have to be emptied of orange wine, made from those mouldy Christmas oranges discarded at the village Post Office and the old shop. Any incomplete bottle has to be consumed at the time, to prevent waste; it is a good excuse and it is a fine wine, strong and conducive to laughter.

For those who do not like wine, elder is still useful, for the flowers can be made into a pleasant elderflower squash. It is made from forty elderflower heads, picked in early bloom, three lemons, four pounds of sugar, and four pints of boiling water. The flowerheads are washed, placed in a bucket with the sugar and sliced lemons, and the water is then poured in. The bucket should be covered and allowed to stand for five days in a cool place, and stirred once a day. The mixture is then strained through muslin and bottled. It can be used immediately, and water is added to it like a normal squash; served cool it is a very refreshing summer drink.

The link between elderberries and birds can best be seen on the recreation ground, for by the bowling green there is a solitary elder bush. Its presence has even been discussed by the Parish Council, and after a heated debate it was eventually decided that a sparrow was responsible for planting it and not members of the bowls club. Now, every so often, the bush is hacked down, but after each attack it always grows up again.

The bowling goes on throughout the summer, and is played mainly by the older men of the village, who water, roll, and cut the green so that the 'woods' run true. The main summer game however is still cricket, but unfortunately the village cricket team was disbanded many years ago, and cost makes it unlikely that it will ever be resurrected. The old heavy roller has disappeared, and where a level square was once layed, the slight undulations of the old ridges and furrows have reasserted themselves. Consequently those who want to play or watch, have to visit some of the surrounding villages, or switch on the television set. The game still gives interest, and the mood and sound of cricket being played on a village green is an integral part of summer.

I play for the next village, and one Saturday afternoon in June we played a typical match out in the fens. The game was 'in the cup', and as the fields became smaller, and even flatter, we knew that we were heading in the right direction. Once in the village an old lady was asked the way to the cricket ground: 'Oh', she replied, 'it's the green field up there on the left.' All the fields were green, with growing potatoes, wheat, barley and carrots, but eventually the one of grass was found. Some of the 'fen tigers' arrived in wellington boots, and one appeared by walking across an adjoining field of potatoes. The village is 'cricket mad' and the club-house-cum-pavilion is far larger than normal, and it also has a bar which was already open and doing trade.

The home side won the toss and decided to bat; it was soon clear why many of them had arrived in wellington boots for parts of the outfield squelched. Wickets immediately began to fall and when the score had reached six runs for three wickets it seemed that we would be home by tea time. At fourteen for four a minor revival began when a tall batsman, with broad shoulders and wearing jeans, began to hit the ball with great power. He was then joined by an older man, 'a tonker', who swung his bat belligerently, as if he was scything or trying to hit a rat with a shovel. Over thirty runs were scored very quickly including three enormous sixes, two of which cleared some tall trees on the boundary, and the other sailed over the club house. In his anxiety to produce something unhittable, one of the bowlers let go of the ball too early. It narrowly missed the square-leg umpire, and must have been one of the widest wides ever bowled. Another towering shot went up almost vertically, but it was quite safe, for the fielder fumbled and dropped it; he was one of those who had visited the bar beforehand and during the course of the innings three players and an umpire had to leave the field for natural reasons, and one had to leave twice. Eventually the stand was over and the whole team was out for a modest seventy.

After a tea of locally grown salad, the runs of our reply came steadily, with the fall of an occasional wicket. When one catch dollied up a player dived full length, but dropped the ball. He had dived in the wrong place, for when he stood up his whites were plastered from head to foot with black fenland mud. Another 'skyer' followed shortly afterwards. Again, it should have been an easy catch, but it went to a bowler who hadn't been bowling.

He ran at it with one hand above his head, only for the ball to fall behind him. 'There', said one of the home supporters, 'he's only ever been known to catch a ball off his own bowling.' It seemed that we must win, and rain was the only thing that could prevent it. Heavy black clouds built up from the south, thunder rumbled menacingly, and rain could be seen falling in sheets. 'You're safe', a local informed us, 'when storms come up from over there they always follow the river.' It grew dark and it seemed as if rain must fall, but sure enough the storm suddenly seemed to change direction and skirted round the village. Victory was ensured with a huge six, and while some players returned to the bar, others went to buy strawberries and potatoes from a nearby house, at a fraction of shop prices.

The 'jungle' is one of the few fields that continues to be enclosed by tall thick hawthorn hedges, brambles and elm trees. It has not been cultivated for many years as it is an area of heavy clay and the drainage pipes of a large field run into it. Elm trees spread out, midway along, to form a small copse, and there is also a public right of way down to the water's edge, for the parish sheep-dip was once dug out next to the main stream. For a short time, after the brook was cleaned out and the spoil was spread all over the field, it lost its wildness, but recently it returned to jungle. Jackdaws nest in the old elms, the undergrowth harbours foxes, and there is a wealth of interesting plants and wildflowers. Their blooming and fading shows the flowering succession of the seasons, and as the months of summer move on towards autumn, so the flowers get higher and higher.

The procession starts in the early spring with the yellow celandine and the coltsfoot, followed by violets, ground ivy and the taller Jack-by-the-Hedge. Yellow rocket is taller still and then cow parsley takes over. Hogweed and hemlock grow upwards into June, with their mass of white inflorescences making an elevated plain several feet from the ground. Insects, bees and butterflies are attracted to them and warblers, flycatchers and even sparrows pursue them in dancing flight. The dog roses flower in clumps and in the hedges, and the mossy robin's pincushions appear in their foliage. Lower down the brilliant yellow of the

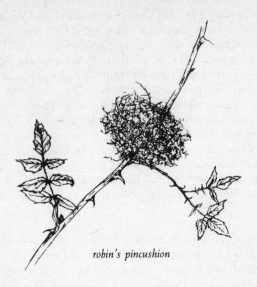

robin's pincushion

meadow vetchling shows, as it uses its entwining tendrils to climb into light, and the blue tufted-vetch climbs even higher. Grasses and sedges add to the variety and later hops, bindweed, and wild angelica complete the summer cycle. It is a pleasant

wild angelica

place to walk, watch and contemplate, and as I sat and rested there one warm afternoon I was pleased to be in the last wild meadow of the parish.

The other place where a variety of wildflowers can be seen undisturbed during the month, is along the old railway line, now the site of a radio telescope. Several times I scrambled down the bank of the bridge to wander along the roadway that has replaced the track. Dog roses, bryony and a few trailing creepers of wild honeysuckle intruded up and over the thorn, and along the verges several flowers grew; bright yellow bird's foot trefoil, black meddick with its small yellow flowers and clover-like leaves, and grasses, several of which held conspicuous globules of 'cuckoo-spit'. Now there are few cuckoos, but the 'spit' has nothing to do with them, for the saliva-like froth conceals the 'cuckoo-spit insect'. It is the nymph of the frog hopper, a small jumping insect that can usually be found in the harvest field. Experts say that in any case the substance is not spit, it is exuded from the opposite extremity, to make a protective covering. Among the grasses too were several pieces of flowering salad burnet, an unusual plant that looks similar to plantain. Its flowers turn from green to scarlet and look rather like raspberries until they burst, when the long stalked stamens give a peculiar hairy appearance.

Late in the month I went to walk in both refuges again, glad that there were still two areas free from spray and people. They had both changed; the jungle had been mowed, to improve the pasture for bullocks, and the old railway line had received the attention of a rotary mower, to make it look tidy. Obviously those who use the telescope to gaze into distant galaxies cannot see the beauty just a few yards away from their own doorsteps.

The fact that rabbits dislike elder is shown by the hedge that grows along a dividing bank between two fields near the rifle range. It is almost at the top of a small hill, and although there are blackthorn bushes and hawthorn trees, where the rabbit population is greatest, elder predominates. The chalky bank is riddled with rabbit holes, and on either side of the hedge the crops are heavily grazed, several yards into the fields. Foxes often convert burrows into earths during the spring, and there are other larger entrances too, for it is in this hedge that the parish's only badger setts can be found. It is astonishing that the badgers remain, for 'night-firing' takes place at the range, attempts are often made to shoot the rabbits, and now, at the bottom of the hill, the new motorway adds to the disturbance. Not surprisingly the animals are cautious and not easy to see, and the problem of watching them is made more difficult by the bank and the eddying wind.

After grass had been flattened near the entrance of one of the holes, I decided to sit outside in the hope of seeing the occupants. I was sure that badgers were present, because a heap of grass was nearby, as if collected for bedding, and there were deep claw marks scored into an elder trunk where claws had been stretched and sharpened. The first two attempts were unsuccessful, indeed the first was a disaster, for after walking carefully along the hedge, to an elder tree, I settled down behind a bush, to watch. Unfortunately it was the wrong tree and I spent two and a half hours sitting outside a collapsed and disused rabbit hole. On the second occasion there was a strong northerly breeze and so I crouched down-wind in some blackthorn. After a few minutes a rabbit emerged from a nearby burrow and almost walked into me; it then sat by its hole for several minutes, periodically thumping its back legs onto the earth in warning. In the silence the thumping seemed almost deafening and I could feel the vibrations. Consequently no badgers emerged.

On the third evening everything was right; it was quiet, still and windless, as I concealed myself close to the correct elder tree, about seven yards away from the sett. The call of a distant cuckoo came faint but clear, it was only the second one I had heard, and although it was June, it had not yet changed its tune. Skylarks and yellowhammers sang, and the grating call of partridges came from a field of wheat. The sounds seemed to clarify with the onset of darkness; moths flew and occasionally I heard the shrill squeak of bats as they hunted above the hedge. Not far from my head I noticed a mass of aphids on a small elder shoot, with black ants crawling all over them. Gradually the full moon appeared and shone brightly and the lights of the road works began to stand out clearly in the fading light. Rabbits moved out of their burrows to graze, and in that still twilight time, between night and day, imagination gave shape and movement to once familiar things.

Suddenly I started, for there just seven yards away was a large badger. It was so close that I held my breath for silence. Books say that badgers leave their setts cautiously, but this one had almost shot out. It was a large animal and the white stripes of its head stood out clearly in the half light. It stopped briefly, stretched, and made off along the bank, where bushes and darkness engulfed it. I breathed again. It was too dark to stay on, for even with the moon shining the leaves threw all the holes into shadow. My ninety minute wait had been rewarded by a five second sighting, but at least I had confirmed that badgers were still in residence, and the memory of the large badger so close will last a lifetime.

July

❧

Daughter of pastoral smells and sights
And sultry days and dewy nights
July resumes her yearly place
Wi' her milking maiden face

THE RAIN SPREAD OVER into July with the last of the hay still lying untouched and wasting in the field. Each day more of the quality was washed from it, and when a fine afternoon did come, smoke drifted skywards from a nearby farm. The farmer had found his hay rotting and mouldy and so instead of using his baler, he simply took out a box of matches and set fire to it. Smoke appeared one afternoon much nearer, for a bulldozer moved into an old orchard, uprooting the trees and hauling them onto a large bonfire. The work went on for most of the month; it was a sad waste of wood, for it would have made excellent logs. It was a waste of life too, for the orchard was overgrown with brambles and high grasses, and numerous birds nests and fledglings must have been crushed. It is strange how outrage is shown at hunting, shooting and fishing, yet acts of destruction where the suffering and pain is much worse, but not so obvious, pass without censor. Death continued on the road as well, with two more hedgehogs and a farmyard cat being flattened.

One morning another victim lay smashed on the verge, close to where Tit Brook flows under the main road. It was a kingfisher, still warm, but quite lifeless, with its ribs crushed and its abdomen ripped open. Blood oozed from its useless beak, but the turqoise feathers were still brilliant, as if daubed on with a painter's brush. As I looked at the crushed body and the shattered life, I remembered the pair I had seen in the spring and felt a mixture of anger, disappointment and sadness.

Other streaks of colour also appeared and warned of imminent death, for the first scorched and shrivelled leaves of Dutch elm disease appeared in the hedgerow elms. The disease usually appears in late June or early July, and it rapidly spread to many parts of the parish, including the spinney and the jungle, apparently picking out trees at random. The cycle is quick and simple; the leaves begin to shrivel, as if scorched by fire, and then they pass through the colours of autumn until they fall and the tree or shrub is quite lifeless.

A few fine days came and John turned what was left of the hay to let it dry out completely; most of the goodness had gone from it, but he baled it, for the cows will eat almost anything if hay and straw are scarce during the winter. One of the most pleasant days was St Swithin's, which was a relief after all the rain, because of the old warning:

> *Oh St Swithin if thou'll be fair,*
> *For forty days it will rain nae mair,*
> *But if St Swithin thou be wet,*
> *For forty days it raineth yet.*

We take St Swithin seriously, and were genuinely relieved when it did not rain. Fine summer weather followed, with fresh strawberries ripening in the garden and the swallows flying high. The occasional pigeon also reflected the mood and the season, flapping lazily but steeply upwards, with its wings slapping together at the height of its climb, to glide down again as if relaxing in the coolness of rushing air. In the garden the roses bloomed, the green of the trees mellowed, and the first of the tortoiseshell butterflies settled on the clump of purple-pink marjoram in front of the kitchen window. As I sat in the afternoon heat, time seemed suspended, and even the insects appeared to hang motionless in the deep lagoons of shade beneath the trees. Young blackbirds, big-beaked and tailless, flapped clumsily and noisily from one perch to another, and the speckled young of robins called to their parents in the apple trees. A similar sound revealed a spotted-flycatcher, flitting out in darting flight to catch an insect, before returning to its perch. It too had young, and several times it took food to a fledgling almost the same size as itself. Fly-catchers are small, pleasant birds that linger on in memory as part of the panoply of high summer. Yet many people do not recognise them, assuming them to be hedgesparrows, or some other small brown bird, and by so doing they miss a summer visitor of great charm and character.

Wild mallow flowered in the garden and along the roadside verges. It is like a small wild hollyhock, which flowers for several weeks. Its success was caused by the local county council which decided not to cut the verges with its normal regularity because of economic cuts. Few people seemed to mind, for the mallow, together with clumps of white campion and yellow melilot, were far more attractive than closely cropped verge.

It was during the hot weather that I saw a swarm of bees. The day had started off with fog, but that soon melted into a fine day, confirming the saying: 'A summer fog is for fine weather.' At first I thought the air was simply shimmering and moving in the heat, but then the buzzing and motion focussed into a swarm of flying bees. Again, from a weather viewpoint it was a good omen, as it is said that: 'Bees will not swarm before a near storm.' For beekeepers the sign was not so good as: 'A swarm in July is not worth a fly.'

As soon as the buds on the garden lime trees burst into fragrant flower, they were quickly found, and at times the trees were actually humming with the sound of working bees, both bumble and honey. Some of the bumblebees flew to a nest in the crumbling brickwork of the old greenhouse; they were attractive creatures, dark, with rich rufous backs. All bees are a delight to watch, and the foxgloves were also worked, with the searching bees disappearing inside the hanging bells. Before gaining entrance to the scented centres of lillies, they had to force themselves past the pollen coated stamens, and so, as nectar was obtained, pollination was assured. The rambler roses set the final touch to the summer garden, as the ash trellises over which they trailed became a mass of red and pink. For me their appearance is always tinged with regret, for they mark the point where summer slowly but visibly moves towards autumn.

After hay cart, work on the farm was far from finished, for the yards were full of 'muck', and John immediately began 'muck cart', already several weeks behind schedule. Father and Charlie began preparing the grain bins for harvest and a neighbouring farmer cut his field of rape, it is an unusual crop, for it has to be cut while green, and left to dry and ripen in the fields, until it is fit for the combine.

One of the cows aborted along the brook meadows, four months before she was due to calve, and as a precaution against brucellosis she was put into isolation. Brucellosis, or 'contagious abortion', is a disease that can produce malarial like symptoms in people, and as the herd is 'brucellosis free', if any cow is found to have the disease, it has to be slaughtered. Fortunately laboratory tests proved negative, and she was allowed back into the herd.

Initially other mothers were more successful with their young, although the first gosling that hatched in March, died for no obvious reason. Two more soon emerged from beneath the scraggy broody hen that was their foster-mother, and like wild adult linnets or warblers, that faithfully feed young cuckoos, so the hen seemed oblivious to the differences in feet, feathers and bill. In true motherly fashion she clucked and cooed to her family and ruffled her feathers and arched her wings to make the dogs and cats keep their distance. At feeding time she would split grains of corn with her beak, inviting her brood to peck at the small pieces. Newly hatched chickens run forward at this particular sight and sound, in instinctive response, but the goslings took little notice and just guzzled down all they could using their beaks like shovels rather than picks. The hen seemed undismayed, and her maternal care did not diminish as her brood grew at an astonishing rate. By the middle of July they were both much larger than she, and fully feathered, but still the three went around the farm-yard and garden together, and every night Father or John shut them inside an old hen house to keep them safe from foxes.

One night, by the time Father reached the henhouse, the old hen had disappeared; she was not roosting outside and she had not found her way back to the rest of the hens, she had simply vanished. The mystery was soon solved, for by dusk on the next evening the white gosling had gone too. The answer came with daylight, for in the middle of the field behind the farm was a patch of white goose feathers, flecked with blood. It was the work of a fox, which had visited before the shed had been shut up. I assumed that it meant the presence of a vixen and her growing cubs.

Soon afterwards I was surprised by the behaviour of a small dark, short-haired cat, for she kept coming into the house, meowing and rubbing herself against our legs as if she was trying to tell us something. It was unusual, for normally she keeps entirely to the farmyard, spending most of her days hunting mice and rats, and only coming to the old granary at feeding time. With her tail erect and meowing loudly, she led us to an old bale

kittenless cat

stack and a hole in the bales. I felt inside; my hand rested on something damp and cold. I pulled out the bodies of three kittens, all dead, and again she meowed as if beseeching us to restore life. All the kittens had their necks broken, one was headless and another had a lump eaten out of its rump. The dogs could not have been responsible, for that part of the bale stack was too insecure, and again it seemed to me that it was the work of a fox. Foxes often remove the heads of hens when they kill, and perhaps the kittens had been left as appetite had been satisfied elsewhere. I buried the kittens, but the cat's sorrow did not cease for several days. On several nights she climbed through my bedroom window, jumping onto my bed wanting fuss and reassurance. Gradually her need for human company and consolation left and her territory again became the farmyard. The lonely gosling was slowly accepted by the other geese, which fortunately meant protection, as well as companionship, for with its hissing aggression, no normal fox will risk a close encounter with a healthy gander.

One morning, late in the month, the dead body of a three-quarters grown cub lay at the side of the road. It confirmed my theory of a vixen and her cubs, and it also confirmed that the car is the most destructive predator to be found in the countryside.

The middle Saturday of the month was the day of the Village Flower Show, one of the best days in the parish calendar, and the only day when people have to pay to get on to the recreation ground. Almost inevitably, a few days before the show, a council flail mower went around the grassy areas of the village, cutting down the wildflowers including a clump of bright blue meadow-cranesbills, near the pond. The marquee was erected and gardeners searched out their potential prize-winners.

The day itself was hot and breezy, and a large crowd gathered in front of an old four-wheeled trailer, decorated as a dais, from which the show was to be declared open. The opening ceremony was performed by a woman who had once lived in the village, but who had moved, with her husband's job, to pastures thought to be greener. She was pleased to be back, she said, and after a short speech John's small daughter, in her Sunday best, was lifted onto the trailer to present a bouquet and a nervous curtsy. The old village greengrocer was then presented with a buttonhole by a young boy. It was a token of appreciation for his work of providing vegetables for the village from his back-room, and for his previous efforts at the flower show; both of which activities had been curtailed by arthritis.

Inside the marquee the vegetables and flowers were laid out

and prizes had been awarded. There were fewer entries than usual because of the cold wet spring, but there were various vegetables including carrots, potatoes, beans and onions. The prize-winning onions were large, but dry, and it seemed likely that they were on a tour of all the local shows to capture the prizes. As an indication of the poor gardening weather there was only one marrow entered, and the first prize was duly awarded. In one of the flower arranging classes there was also just a single entry, but strangely, that was awarded second prize, presumably to encourage a better effort next year. There were small flowers, large flowers, unusual vegetables, and among all the carefully washed and prepared exhibits was a solitary bunch of dirty radishes. The largest entry was for home-made wine, with over sixty bottles on display, although there was no sign of the judge who was said to have tasted every one. Outside there were stalls selling cakes, groceries and a variety of household goods; a bottle stall offered an assortment of bottles from whisky to tomato ketchup, as prizes for a lucky ticket, and there was a competition for threading cotton reels on string in thirty seconds.

By the time all the bottles had been won, and the cotton reels threaded, the children were ready to enter their races; egg and spoon, sack, three-legged and wheelbarrow. The unclaimed produce was auctioned off and the marquee was cleared ready for the evening's entertainment of drinking, eating over-done barbecued beef-burgers, and listening to folk songs. It was a good day, when villagers from the High Street, the new estates, and from neighbouring parishes, all mingled together. The only note of misery came from some members of the Horticultural Society committee, who complained about the price of hiring the marquee and warning that 'this flower show could be the last one held under canvas.' The warning is generally accepted as a good sign, for each year it is given, and so far it has been wrong every time.

The most interesting 'flower show' of the month was offered free, along Church Lane, for the council workmen still had not been to remove the 'weeds'. The churchyard and vicarage walls had patches of lichen and moss mottling the brickwork, as well as

straggling arms of ivy. There was even a clump of yellow flowering fumitary, somehow drawing moisture from its precarious
elevated hold. At the side, ivy-leaved toadflax flourished where
life would be impossible for most plants, with its trailing stems,
its miniature ivy-shaped leaves, and small pansy-like flowers.
Close by, among the less welcome ground ivy and barley grass
were perfectly formed real wild pansies, the 'heartsease', a
flower of love. The petals were the texture of velvet, a deep
royal purple, with yellow honey guides directing to a centre of
gold. Around one of the churchyard gates, more yellow flowers
grew, with clumps of greater celandine and herb bennet. The
celandines were a mixture of short and tall, with those growing
in good soil reaching over three feet in height, and those growing
from the brickwork struggling to about a foot. The flowers were
delicate, almost fragile in appearance, and their presence is a
reminder that most parishes grew them at one time, for the
bright orange sap can be used to cure both warts and ring worm.

The churchyard itself has flowers of its own, quite independent
from the wreaths and remembrance roses, for in wild corners
herb robert can be found, a foul smelling plant whose pleasant
pink flowers can be seen for most of the summer. Self-heal, a
small nettle-like 'herb', grows in 'the churchyard sod', and that
too was once used in country medicine; the small purple flowers
are attractive and remind me of bumblebees. Pink and white
Dove's-foot cranesbills also flourish along one side, together
with a large clump of another type of cranesbill that the flower
books claim should not be growing there at all.

It is surprisingly pleasant and peaceful to stroll around the
churchyard, and together with the school, the church, the Hoops,
and the vicarage, it forms the old centre of the village.

During the month the Minister of the Baptist church left, but a
new vicar moved into the vicarage and people were eager to see
him, to size him up and assess his chances of success: 'Just what
the village wants', one old sage concluded, 'he was a prison
chaplain before he came here, so he's in the right place. The
vicarage has even got a wall round it, so he should feel at home.'

All through the month work on the new motorway, along one

side of the parish boundary, proceeded at an almost frenetic pace. Thirty-one ton earth movers and scrapers, like giant earth eating animals with insatiable appetites, tore up the soil. They hauled their loads to where a bridge and an interchange were being constructed, and disgorged their contents to form a new hill. The drivers bounced along in their cabs, followed by clouds of white dust, and they were joined by men on bulldozers and in Land Rovers. The road workers talk with pride about their work, as if they are pioneers opening up a new country. They seem oblivious to the fact that they are changing the land and the parish, and there is no concern that the area of the interchange is as large as the village itself. They do not talk in acres, feet and inches, but in hectares and metres and they measure the accuracy of their bridges to a fraction of a millimetre. Where the motorway crosses the main road to the town, temporary traffic lights check the flow of cars and lorries to allow the earth movers to continue their work uninterrupted. On several sunny days the traffic light operator sat with his shirt off, and every time a mechanical monster roared past he was engulfed in dust, for although the road is being built with great technical skill, they had placed the traffic light controls down wind of the work, and they hadn't the common sense to move them. As the clouds cleared, so the shovelless operator would walk backwards and forwards across the road, kicking away lumps of clay. Then at last he would change the lights to green and the queues of commuters and salesmen would continue on their way.

The great scar of the road skirts the slight hill of the badger setts, and then bends away to the brook, and to the river where the otters were seen earlier in the year. The engineers and road builders see it as 'progress', for 'it will last fifty years and you will be able to get to London twenty minutes quicker.' The farmer by the rifle range who has had forty acres taken for the road is not impressed: 'If they can get to London so quick, then I wish they would all go there', is his comment. Some of the villagers welcome the road, but most of the old residents of the parish see it as an eye sore of mud and concrete that has been imposed on the land regardless of local feelings and needs. They can see no sense in spending millions of pounds to allow them to get to a place that they have no desire to visit, and it seems strange to close a railway, and then construct roads to cater for the displaced traffic. Some of the older men also survey the scene with great sadness, for the interchange covers the site of an old 'turnpike' road to Grantchester, where a drinking trough stood beneath a large willow tree. It was along that road, in the past, that they drove their horse drawn carts and waggons full of corn, for grinding at the ancient water mill; but the old road junction is now unrecognisable.

The one person really to welcome the road is the publican at the White Horse, for every day at dinner time and in the evenings, men from the road call in. Many of the pipe-layers and labourers are itinerant Irish workers who travel from site to site, drinking and working hard as they go. The Irish are easy to identify for they are brawny men with low slung belts and bulging stomachs that advertise the size of their alcoholic intake. To cater for the demand, draught Guinness has been installed in the pub, and many of the workers average as many as twelve pints a night. At one time, to save a long walk from the site, one would arrive driving his JCB digger, while others would summon a taxi.

Occasionally some would arrive already drunk at opening time, having spent the afternoon drinking illegally in an 'Irish' pub in the town, a fact known to almost everybody, except the police. On occasions Murphy arrived so drunk that he had to lean against the wall to play darts. One evening he objected to people watching him as he swayed; he shuffled up to one and said:'If you keep looking at me I'll kick your bloody head in.' 'Go on then', came the confident reply, for if Murphy had taken one foot off the ground he would have fallen flat on his face.

Since the Water Authority decided to turn the brook into an efficient drainage channel, rather than retain it as a wilderness of running water, pools, overhanging boughs and natural dams, its character has changed, but it still has some beauty and it continues to form a more pleasant roadway through the parish.

Ducks, herons and kingfishers fly along its meandering course, swallows skim over it for flies, foxes hunt along its banks, and moorhens leave their footprints in the mud under the bridge.

Other footprints, too, occur from time to time, as men from the water authority follow the example of others and cut down the willow saplings, grasses and wildflowers that grow on the banks. It is a pity, for several attractive plants have re-established themselves since the brook was 'cleaned out'. The small marsh-forget-me-not grows at the water's edge, and the old 'wound-herb', comfrey is quite common. Some find it so attractive that it is grown in many cottage gardens and because of the shape of its flowers it is known as 'church-bells'. In addition there is water-cress, fool's watercress and brooklime, which is another plant that looks and tastes like watercress, except for its blue 'bird's eye' flowers. Meadowsweet, hemlock, hemp agrimony, catmint, fleabane, and banks of great hairy willowherb, are all to be found, but many things are still absent after the destruction; the 'pokers' of the great reedmace, the 'flags' of the yellow iris, and the once common wild waterlillies have all gone. Otters remain only in the memories of old men and even the once common reed-buntings are seldom seen. Before the arrival of the drag-lines, these 'bearded' little birds were common, because of the cover given by the rushes and reeds, but each year since, their numbers have declined, and I have not found a nest for two consecutive summers.

On a warm humid evening I walked along the banks hoping to see a bunting and signs of young, but again their old favourite sites were deserted. At intervals, three herons were hunting; they were the first I had seen since the winter, probably indicating that the young had been successfully reared and the heronries dispersed, for the birds to resume their solitary wandering lives. There was plenty of food for them; miller's thumbs, on the mud, and sticklebacks too, with the cocks still sporting their bright red breasts of the breeding season.

At a bend, where watermint was flowering, the first damsel flies were darting over the water; they seemed to be charged-up with solar energy and glowed the colour of polished copper. Small fish broke the stillness as they rose for flies, and warblers, on light, fanning wingbeats, fluttered between two raised patches of reeds, to feed their young. A water spider walked over the surface with complete assurance, and near me a clump of marsh-woundwort hung over the water. The flowers were a rich

water mint

mauve, and where they competed with grasses they looked just like late orchids showing through.

As I headed for home a moorhen splashed noisily from a clump of rushes; concealed within was a woven nest containing seven blotched eggs. A few days later she was disturbed again, when men from the water authority returned with their scythes. For no apparent reason all the cover, including the comfrey and wound-wort, was cut down. The reeds with the young warblers were flattened and the moorhen's nest was completely exposed. Not surprisingly, within a day the eggs had vanished, no doubt stolen by a fox, a heron, a crow, or a small boy.

It was at about this time too that I followed the brook down to the Cam, to look upstream for the otters that had again been reported. That part of the river was peaceful and full of fish, with banks of reeds giving shelter to the surface of the water. The water meadows held cattle, grazing contentedly with their tails

the river bridge

swishing and flicking at flies. The bridge was half hidden by foliage and the scene was that of a traditional English lowland landscape. It was an illusion though, for the otters were still absent
and the new road was more intrusive. In addition the air near the
bridge was pungent and heavy with the odour of weedkillers and
insecticide, for it is close to a factory where agricultural sprays
are made.

August

Harvest approaches with its bustling day
The wheat tans brown and barley bleaches grey
In yellow garb the oat land intervenes
And tawney glooms the valley thronged with beans

MORE HEAVY SHOWERS FELL in the early part of the month. It was after one, with water still dripping from the overhanging willows, that I found another late moorhen's nest, in a clump of reeds near Tit Brook. For some reason it had been overlooked by the Water Authority men and contained five eggs. As I turned to leave it in peace, Nellie blundered through the water after me, capsizing the nest and cracking an egg. Inside the small moorhen was curled up, perfectly formed and breathing through its beak; it was obviously about to hatch. I carefully restored the nest and the damp eggs, and hoped that the mother would not forsake. Two days later the eggs had vanished, but among the matted reeds were small fragments of shell, showing that the eggs had not been stolen, but had hatched. Later on in the month I saw the black fluffy brood on several occasions and they appeared to be doing well.

Chicks of a different sort arrived on the farm, for due to a 'computer error' one hundred and twenty-five day-old cockerels arrived a fortnight late. They were white, downy and attractive, and were placed under the warmth of an infra-red lamp, with food and water, to start them growing towards Christmas. Other hatching also took place, for the white broken shell of a wood pigeon's egg betrayed its stick nest and late young. Several times a pigeon cooed in the garden weeping willow tree and the mixture of short and long cooes is said to be a recitation of:

A little Jenny wren lays ten, ten, ten,
But I can lay only twoo, twooo, twooo.

August is also a traditional month for flowers, with yarrow along the roadsides and the teasles by the brook glowing with flame-blue heads. Thistles attracted many tortoiseshell butterflies along the banks, and wild angelica flowered in the damp. They attracted many insects, particularly flies, hover flies, and 'blood-suckers', the red soldier-beetles that seem to spend most of their time locked in passion, whether on leaves, flowers, or even in

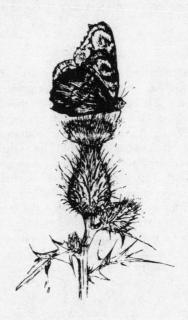

butterfly on flowering thistle

mid-air. Sprays of soft pink blackberry blossom draped the older hedgerows, and they too drew butterflies, bumblebees, honey bees, hover flies and blow flies with bodies of an incandescent metallic green. Spiders, ladybirds, earwigs, and even snails with light, striped shells joined them among the foliage.

In a cottage garden close to the farm another flower attracted many insects. It was a great mullein, with a lengthy spike of yellow flowers, and at seven feet high, it still seemed to be growing. I first noticed its large leaves in January, and with each month it gradually grew, until mid-summer, when it accelerated upwards like a wild hollyhock. Sometimes the plant attracts the caterpillars of the mullein moth, a type that seems to thrive on the large hairy leaves. But none appeared and the leaves were uneaten; they were not picked either, although at one time they were popular in herbal tobaccos.

In the garden, real hollyhocks and policeman's helmets flowered, while the pink flowers of bindweed attracted butterflies, giving a soft blend of colour and gentleness, almost as if their long tongues were drinking from specially moulded cups. Flock formed a swaying border of white and the hebes continued in seemingly perpetual bloom. They are small evergreen shrubs from New Zealand, with a mass of buddleia-like flowers. They were again popular with butterflies and bees, and among the leaves of one was a large spider's web of impressive size and construction. Its threads channelled insects into a funnelled interior, where the shrivelled up bodies told of success; it was rather like a miniature trap used by fen eel-catchers, and in the past similar constructions must have been the inspiration to old fishermen.

As the crops ripened, the fields turned yellow and gold, and the harvest flowers told of the season. In some places poppies gave the look of earlier harvests and when picked by John's two small children, Edwin and Lena, they were warned, like countless other country children before them, not to smell the flowers for fear of headaches. It is a long held belief, but strangely one that is seldom seen recorded, although in one of John Clare's poems he writes:

> Corn poppys that in crimson dwell
> Calld 'headachs' from their sickly smell.

Their reappearance was caused by the cool late spring, for many farmers sprayed their crops before the poppy seeds had germinated, and so once again the fields assumed their old harvest colour. Past the gypsies in the drift, the ditches and farm

field scabious

tracks still had wild carrots, parsnips, field scabious, mayweed and knapweed growing. In the old days the scabious was far from welcome for its tough stems slowed the harvest by blunting scythes.

Didecoys had returned to the drift, and from the heaps of iron and scrap, their harvest had already started. Five caravans were there, and the nearby farmers were far from pleased. In the old shop a smallholder complained that one of his wheat fields had been transformed into an open latrine: 'It's terrible, they're all over the fields with their dogs after hares. What's left of the hedges should be cut down completely, so that when the wind is right we can burn the stubble and set fire to the lot.' Bert behind the counter agreed, for a few days before a didecoy boy had been in to buy sweets with a one pound note. On being given his change he demanded more, claiming that he had paid with a 'fiver'. Bert showed him the door.

Two more hedgehogs were killed on the main road, during the same night and within a yard of each other; but in the cottage garden by the old village pump, there was another with six half-grown young. On two consecutive Sunday afternoons I found a dead mole in the brook meadows, and each one had a broken neck. They had just been left after death and it seemed to me that a fox had probably caught and killed them, but had found them unpleasant to eat, rather like a cat after killing a shrew. Another casualty was a bat, that John found, it was a small pipistrelle, and he sent the body away for analysis. The reply came back that it was a young one, and it had probably died of starvation because of the earlier cold and wet. Adult bats live for up to twenty years, and the young are born at the end of June or at the beginning of July. They are suckled for about a month, but this juvenile had obviously not been able to manage on its own. Each year the bats fly on summer evenings, but we never see where they come from, and we have never found them hanging upside down or hibernating.

As the month wore on the damp weather demanded patience, for with a few days of sun, the first corn would be ripe, and harvest could begin. During the period of waiting John pulled up a row of small hawthorn bushes that divided the grass field behind the farm into two. It was not a properly planted hedge, but showed where sparrows had perched on the barbed wire fence after eating hawthorn berries. At last the weather changed, and after three days of fine weather harvest began. We started with winter oats, and soon all the farms were busy combining, carting grain and baling straw. The twenty-fourth was fine, which after the wet promised well; for:

> *If St Bartholomew's Day be fair and clear,*
> *Then a prosperous autumn comes that year.*

Several long and hard days followed, made harder one evening by the cows getting into the cuckoo barley. But then stubble burning started, and as the smoke drifted upwards, so clouds seemed to form and thunder and rain came. It is a sequence that I have noticed for several years, and it is one that sends Foss running home to let herself into the house for protection. Additional signs of change were just perceptible, as a new coolness lingered on in the early morning. Others too felt the movement of seasons, for a wheatear stayed briefly by the brook, before moving on, and one afternoon a large flock of feeding swallows passed over, moving steadily southwards, several weeks earlier than usual.

Harvest is still an enjoyable time in the farming calendar, but its pace has quickened as its nature has changed. Some of the hard physical labour has gone, but the long hours remain, and on a fine day work will continue until the dampness of dusk. It is noisy, dusty work around the combine, and masks have to be worn, as they do when the grain is emptied into the trailer and when it is augered into the bins in the barns. Mechanisation has not made the work more leisurely, in fact it has transformed harvest into a time of rushing effort and activity, to get the corn in while the weather holds. In the old days crops could be cut when damp, and left to dry-out in the shocks (stooks), or even in the stacks (ricks), but now a 'high moisture content' can cause the grain to heat up in the bins and spoil, and if there is rain about, harvest can be a time of great anxiety.

But although the days are long and dirty, the diminishing acreage of standing corn is a visual encouragement to work on. Several days we worked for over fifteen hours, finishing dirtier than miners, but with no extra pay, for on a small family farm there is no clocking on or off. Several times I walked back home from Warners Corner after a full day in the half-light of dusk; the quietness of the evening and the absence of engines working made a calming contrast to the noise and the activity of harvest. The stillness was intensified by the absence of birdsong, for the season of breeding, feeding and defending families and territory was finally over. But the feelings of harvest are pleasant, fatigue is mixed with satisfaction, and the rewards are a good appetite, flagons of cider, and a sound night's sleep.

John drove the combine, cutting ten foot swathes and leaving rows of battered straw behind him. Going with the wind he would be covered with dust, his face hidden behind a mask, and his dark glasses offering scant protection to his eyes, which at the end of each day were red and stinging. Charlie remained at the barns to shovel and to prepare the corn bins, by lining them with paper; I drove the tractor and trailer to and from the combine, and Father was left free to milk the cows. The only respite each afternoon came when Ellen, John's blonde Swedish wife, brought coffee and sandwiches, which we ate sitting in the straw. Edwin and Lena came with her to ride on the mound of grain in the trailer, the wheat, barley or oats covering their naked legs, and getting into their sandals, as they watched cream coloured caterpillars and earwigs. They were absorbing new experiences in the long endless days of childhood.

The oats were harvested first; they had been 'direct drilled', the autumn before, with no ground cultivation, but they were not a success, with barley from the previous crop competing with them. We will not try that method again until the techniques have been improved. Wheat was next, and as the area of standing corn grew smaller, pheasants and partridges were forced to fly to safety. It was soon apparent that they had experienced a bad nesting season, and because of the cold and wet several pairs were in the process of rearing second broods, after the failure of the first. Two covies of partridges each containing five half-grown young, flew low over the stubble, and one pair had just a solitary chick. There were several families of pheasants too, with the largest containing only six chicks, and as the wheat was almost finished, the mother called her small but feathered brood away from the corn and the combine to skulk in the straw.

In the grass field near the cuckoo barley, John found a partridge chick still covered with down, and small enough to have sat comfortably in a desert spoon. While in the barley itself the dogs put up five small pheasants, just big enough to flutter, squeaking further into the cover. There too was a small trailing plant with tiny yellow and black flowers; it was the round-leaved fluellen. Its presence in the barley was unexpected, as the field had been down to grass for about ten years, and so the

round leaved fluellen

dormant seeds must have been triggered into germination by disturbance. The small red flowers of the scarlet pimpernel also showed up brightly, promising more fine weather, and there were several wild white pansies.

wild pansy or heartsease

As I drove the tractor and trailer by the spinney, one afternoon, I saw a strange movement that stumbled over a ditch and made for the corn. I did not recognise the creature, for it appeared to have feathers, more than four legs, and a furry tail. When I got quite close I stopped the tractor, but I still could not identify the feathered animal. It stopped, aware of my presence, and the feathers swayed; the tail had a conspicuous black tip, and two alert eyes observed me. It was a stoat that had been dragging a pigeon, larger than itself; fear dominated, it dropped the bird and ran off towards the standing wheat.

Half the corn was cut and baling was started. The rest was still to ripen, and then the rain returned.

In addition to harvest the month was also a busy one for the cows. On the very first day the young cattle in the brook meadows were 'gadding'. Galloping around with their tails held high, showing the presence of the warble, or 'gad' fly. It is an unpleasant insect, laying its eggs on the legs of the cattle and apparently causing them some pain; indeed, if a high pitched blow is made at this time of year, it is possible to make the cattle 'gad', even when there is no fly present. When the larvae hatch they eat through the skin and work their way up the body, until they come to rest under the skin of the animal's back, where they make a small breathing hole which causes much discomfort; if the tell-tale swelling is found it can be squeezed and the maggot squirts out. To save animals this unpleasantness they were driven to the farm and treated with fly spray.

The next day as I got up and looked out of the window, I noticed all the cows lying down in the field, a sign of rain, and sure enough within half an hour drizzle started. When the cows were roused, to be called up to the farm for milking, one remained down. It was flat out, unconscious, and only just breathing. When cows lie flat, because of their digestive system, they cannot pass wind and they become 'blown'. The cow was both blown and calving, and father called me and John to try and roll her over, to get the calf out and to release the wind. As we got there she died; there was nothing we could do, just watch as life ended. To save digging a large hole, normally we would have phoned the local beagle kennels to make use of the body, but this time the 'knacker' was phoned to see if we could get some money for pet food; for a cow worth five hundred alive, well and in milk, we were given eight pounds.

Each day too the cows had to be driven to and from Warners Corner for grazing and milking. As they hurried along one morning a helpful motorist started to drive them back, thinking that they had got out, while one afternoon a supercilious, smartly dressed stranger stopped his car and got out. 'Is anyone on point duty?' he asked, 'you are supposed to have somebody at the front as well as the back, I'm reporting you to the police.' Father ignored him, for as far as he was concerned the cows knew their own way and could have managed by themselves, and in any case two people could never be spared at harvest time simply to get the cows. That evening two policemen called, but they were understanding: 'We've got to come as we've had a complaint, but don't worry about it as the cows are no trouble.'

Towards the end of the month two more cows were down

with milk fever, although the calves were alive and well. Nobody seemed to know why, whether it was the season, the diet, or what. They were so bad that Williams was called and he sent a new lady assistant, who injected both animals, and we hoped for recovery. It was a bad day all round for the two tractors broke down, one with clutch trouble and the other with a puncture. The following day both animals were still down and Williams was again summoned; as he walked across the yard with a bottle of calcium in his hands one of the cows got up and walked away; 'There you are', he said, 'that's the way to cure cows.' He was not so fortunate with the other, for although the milk fever had been cured, it seemed as if she had developed paralysis in her back legs and could not stand.

As he considered what to do we discussed injections, for we normally inject cows with milk fever in the neck, but the new female vet had stuck the animals in the ribs. I told Williams of a young dentist I had recently met, who claimed that when administering his first anaesthetic, he had pushed the needle through his patient's cheek and into his own thumb: 'That's nothing,' Williams responded dismissively, 'When I had just started, a woman brought me her horrible little geriatric dog to be put down – we call it wuffanasia. I told her to put it on the table, but she insisted on holding the bloody thing cradled in her arms. Then, just when I went to put the needle in the dog, she moved, and I got her in the left tit. I saw blood coming so I quickly pulled it out and stuck it in the dog. As soon as she saw that she fainted and fell over the electric fire. My boss was very understanding, he said: "First of all you almost kill her, and then you try to set fire to her."'

He could give no guarantee of a cure for the cow, but left a metal clamp to be screwed tightly over her hip bones, twice a day, and then fixed to the tractor's hydraulic muck-loader. She could then be hoisted up and her back legs massaged. It was a difficult and time consuming operation, as the clamp kept sliding off, but it was eventually achieved. She made little progress however, and as soon as the clamp and loader began to lower her, she again crumpled into a heap.

Trouble came to the village too, for two more of the old villagers died, and other people had a number of lesser problems. In the High Street there were complaints about gates, chimneys and mould in some of the council houses, and along the main road there were problems with drains and speeding traffic. The traffic problem was highlighted when a resident was shunted down the road in his car as he went to turn into his gate.

On a small estate of expensive private houses there were also problems, for at the garage, almost opposite, permission was obtained to run a small site for touring caravans during the summer months. The planning application was advertised, discussed by the Parish Council and approved by the District Council. It was only then that the residents organised themselves into action, when it was already too late. They argued that the caravans would be unsightly, that turning vehicles would create traffic hazards, that the visitors themselves would be in danger from the petrol tanks, and that it would bring undesirable elements into the village. The arguments were significant, for they were almost identical to the ones used by the village when the estate itself was first proposed; that the houses, of lavatorial brick, would be unsightly, that the estate would be on the main road, and that it would attract people into the village who would not want to take part in village life. Time has proved most of the fears to have been unfounded, but the newcomers were not to be appeased. Charlie could not understand what all the fuss was about: 'Are the people of the new estate complaining because they will have to look out on to caravans? I would have thought it would have been the other way round.'

A sight of a more unusual nature took place on one of the new estates just as people were going to work, for as one commuter drove off, his wife stood at the garden gate, waving goodbye stark naked. The postman couldn't believe his eyes: 'I'm only showing off my sun tan', she said, and then as an after-thought she added, 'we are moving soon'. 'Oh', he replied, 'it looks as if you've packed your clothes already.' Within a few days variations of the story had circulated the whole village, for gossip is still an enjoyable element of village life.

When Fred killed himself, that too went round the village very quickly, but the story gave no feelings of pleasure or amusement. Although to those who met him, Fred always had a smile, yet beneath his mask he bore much sadness. A few years earlier his wife had died, and then his old black gun-dog had been put down through illness. Problems at work followed, leaving him unemployed, and then trouble with relations had left him feeling useless and desolate and no one seemed to care. On the day of his death he left notes in conspicious places, telling where to find his body and what to do with his house. He left his front door open, and after saying goodbye to his elderly neighbour, he phoned for the police and an ambulance. A shot was heard and groans came from the bottom of his garden. As a friend went to dial 999 the police arrived and the note on the door told them where to go; Fred had bent over his twelve-bore shot gun and blown his heart out.

There was another story that circulated the village, but that turned out to be totally false, and concerned a family of ducks that suddenly appeared on the village pond. Hopes for a brood had risen early in the year, when a pair of mallards had settled, and it seemed a likely place for a nest. Almost inevitably the female was run over by a passing car, and after a few days of solitude the drake flew away. Then later, a mother duck suddenly appeared with eleven ducklings. Some people said she had hatched them from a nest nearby, and others claimed that the brood had been reared in captivity and released. However they got there they were welcome, and were an added attraction to the pensioners and mothers with children, as they went to the nearby post office.

Everything went well until a group of volunteer conservationists arrived one Sunday to clean the pond out. As the human pond cleaners waded in, so the ducks walked out, and their arrival onto the footpath coincided with the approach of a party of ramblers. The ducks then proceeded to waddle ahead of the walkers and they were driven out of the village. When the Parish Clerk saw the spectacle, he set off in pursuit, heading them off at the village boundary. He drove them back, via two fields and a farmyard moat, and eventually they arrived back on the pond.

After that, the ducks grew quickly, until it was difficult to tell the young ones from their mother. On most days pensioners from the old peoples' bungalows would arrive with bread to feed them: 'Do you know those ducks lift their old heads up and jump for tit-bits just like dogs?' Even the gypsies watched them, and contrary to all predictions the pond was not poached.

Then came a day when the pond was deserted, and all the ducks had disappeared. There were many explanations: 'They've been stolen': 'The gypsies have had them after all': 'They've walked to the moat', and 'Somebody's poured paraffin into the pond to frighten them off.' At first glance the last possibility

mother duck

appeared to be the most likely, for there was a large film of oil over part of the pond. But nobody had thrown it in, it was merely road run-off that had washed in after a heavy shower of rain. The old men were genuinely upset by the disappearance and there was much concern.

The answer was simple however, and came one evening as I was walking to the recreation ground for football practice. I heard quacking and looked up to see a group of ducks wheeling round over the trees of the vicarage. Their wings were held open with adjustments for angle and wind-speed, and they seemed to fall almost chaotically out of the air – towards the pond. On several days they came and went, for they had simply learned to fly and so had gained their freedom.

September

Harvest awakes the morning still
And toils rude groups the valley fill
Deserted is each cottage hearth
To all life save the crickets mirth

SEPTEMBER BROUGHT WARM SULTRY DAYS, with a haze made heavier by the smoke of burning stubble. In the next village more than stubble burnt, for a long hedge was devastated, with the leaves scorched and the trunks charred, but in the main there were fewer hedges burnt through negligence than usual. In the mornings, dew clung onto the spiders' webs and the colours of autumn gradually seeped into the verges, hedgerows and fields. There were duns, greys, browns and shades of bronze, all mixing with fading green. The seeding grasses dried to the colour of hay, the hemlock by the brook bleached to a skeletal grey, and clumps of dock and sorrel were the texture and colour of crumbling rust. Rose leaves were edged with autumn and began to curl, the bryony vines held vivid orange fruits and the dog roses and hawthorns became bright with hips and haws. The only berries not to show were those of the elder, for as soon as they turned to blackcurrant ripeness the sparrows ate them greedily, and what they overlooked, people with plastic buckets collected for wine. The shadow of the weeping willow tree stretched longer over the lawn and every day the scarlet Worcester apples became more vivid.

In the meadows the down of thistle heads spilled over into the wind and they were joined by countless crane-flies with dangling legs and gossamer wings. The 'daddy-long-legs' seemed to be everywhere, showing that many 'leather-jackets' had been missed by the rooks and starlings earlier in the year. During the month the movements of the rooks were erratic. Occasionally they returned to the rookery and one windy afternoon they were all feeding in the grass of the brook meadows, but whether they were catching the crane flies as they emerged from the soil in metamorphosis, was not clear. When the birds flew, they began to wheel, dive, and tumble in the air, almost as if they were playing in the warm wind; a kingfisher was engaged in a much more serious task, as it sat on a fallen twig just six inches above the water and the wind-whipped ripples, but its watch was in vain.

The early part of the month was a time of waiting, as the rest of the harvest ripened. A new tractor, at least new to us, was driven into the farmyard on a lorry; it was clean, with a wind-proof cab, power-steering, an almost floating seat to reduce the impact of bumps, and the strength of seventy-five horses. One of the old tractors was taken away, but unlike in the days of real horse-power, there was no emotion with the change, for it was seen as a straightforward business transaction, although it did mean that twenty young cattle had to be loaded up for market, to prevent the bank overdraft from becoming too large. It is strange how farmers still see their deals almost as a form of barter, with the cost of a new tractor, drill, or even a plastic bucket, being measured in tons of wheat, cattle, or dozens of eggs. The purchase also showed something more; it demonstrated the pressure on farming to become more intensive, for the value of its produce increases more slowly than that of industrial goods. Experts have estimated that now it costs one hundred and ten thousand gallons of milk to buy a seventy-five horsepower tractor, whereas just five years ago it took thirty-three thousand gallons.

Each day too the paralysed cow had to be lifted and massaged, but she made no progress, and when Father and Foss drove the cows out of the yard each morning, she would try desperately to stand, hauling herself forward on her front legs, until exhausted. After a fortnight Williams conceded that it was no use to continue and the 'knacker' was called. He shot her where she lay, bled her, and then hauled her onto his lorry, to be taken to the slaughter house for meat. It was a miserable day, for we had fed her, watered her and given her every care, but nothing more could be done.

As the fine weather continued we followed the progress of the harvest on the side of a low limestone hill, to the south of the parish. Gradually the bright golden squares of ripe uncut corn changed to alternate rows of darker stubble, and combined straw. Then smouldering blackness spread over some of the fields, before furrows of freshly turned soil began to appear in readiness for autumn sowing.

After several windy days the grain hardened in the ear and the next piece of wheat was ready, although no sooner had we started than the combine engine cut out with a fuel blockage. It took half an hour to clear and in that time clouds began to build up in the west and the silvery backs of willow and blackberry leaves warned of the approach of rain. We worked as fast as possible, with one eye on the weather and the other on the diminishing area of wheat. With just half an hour's work left, the rain came down in sheets. I emptied the trailer and augered the grain to safety, and then, dripping, I ran to help John cover the combine. But at least we were luckier than one of our neighbours who had his combine battery stolen and so he had a much later start.

Fortunately the next day was bright, and although still damp we finished the wheat, with the grain being ground the same day for cattle food. Harvest continued as a hit and run affair, with combining and days of drying, and ploughing and baling filling the interludes. Mists hung on in the mornings and in the evenings stubble fires burnt brightly like numerous encampments in an unclaimed land. Smoke and smuts drifted down for days, leading to complaints in the local paper from people whose cars and swimming pools had been dirtied and whose priorities obviously did not include the production of food. Some of the combined barley started to heat, due to dampness, and the barn took on the smell of an oast house. It was augered into a ventilation bin and an old Armstrong-Siddley engine, retrieved from an obsolete combine, drove a fan to dry it out.

Warm days returned, and on two of them Father and Charlie saw a bat flying at mid-day. Along the brook and ditches white whisps of willow herb seeds floated by, and the bright yellow of flowering hawkweed and bristly ox-tongue retained a summer freshness. The leaves of the silver birches began to fall, the swallows collected in lines on the telephone wires, and the crane flies continued to drift with the thistle down.

With three days of the month to go, the 'cuckoo barley', although flattened and battered by wind and rain, was at last ripe. We combined its eight acres in a day, and again we worked against a steady build up of cloud. It did not yield well, but at dusk we finished, and harvest was over for another year; we were thankful, and we did not mind the rain that fell the next day.

When the combine leaves a field, the work has not finished, for with cattle, the straw has to be baled for winter fodder and bedding, and the remaining stubble has to be burnt to make autumn ploughing and drilling easier. Baling is another noisy dusty job, with the bales being left in groups for carting. Several times I took the dogs with me as I went to heap bales, making small stacks of seventeen so that the tractor, with its special lifters, could collect one heap at the front and one at the back, to carry them to the farm. As the stacks get higher the work gets hotter and harder, but it is pleasant and even Charlie, at well over seventy, helps, the main reward being the satisfaction of seeing the Dutch barn stuffed full of bales and ready for winter.

Heaping the bales is also warm physical work, but that too is enjoyable, and when the work is finished the heaped bales give the fields an ancient look, reminiscent of stone circles and sun worship. Leather gloves are usually worn, to prevent the strings from blistering the hands, and often as a bale is moved sleek harvest mice with wide brown eyes run for cover. They disappear under straw or into cracks in the ground and the dogs dig and sniff excitedly. Under some bales, compact nests have already been made of woven straw, and with all the animal and mechanical hazards, it is astonishing that any mice survive at all.

Other dangers exist in the fields, and foxes betray their presence by relieving themselves on the bales. It is strange behaviour, but useful, for the 'scats' reveal the fox's harvest diet: small bones, blackberry pips and the indigestible wings of black beetles. They show how the fox's fancy varies from season to season, according to taste or the ease of scavenging. Once the heaps have been built, small patches of plucked feathers are also found on them, together with pellets containing fragments of bone, fur, feathers, and again the wings of black beetles, for kestrels are also in the parish.

It is good to see the kestrels back over the stubbles, and the old country names of windhover and hover-hawk, accurately describe their method of hunting. During the sixties they disappeared, when insecticide seemed to kill off many hawks and falcons, but kestrels have returned and their numbers are almost back to their old levels. On a warm afternoon as I was heaping bales I watched one hovering quite high as it hunted. When a family of linnets or finches flew below, it fell, with its wings held up and its talons down. The small birds scattered and flew off in alarm as the kestrel struck, but it missed its meal. The most spec-

kestrel

tacular hunting occurred on a windswept evening as I worked in a small field by the brook, for the kestrel was hovering and hunting over a rough garden. I stopped working to watch, for it was remarkable as its tail and wings fanned and feathered repeatedly, feeling, searching, holding and repelling the air, to remain static in the wind. At times it dropped to within six feet of the ground, before falling again, but whether the victim was a beetle or a mouse I could not see. After several dives it accelerated upwards and wheeled away in a wide sweeping arc, simply by holding its wings open. It began to circle one of the dishes of the radio telescope and its mewing soon brought another onto the wing. Both then perched in the high steel frame. The numerous ledges would make ideal nesting sites; next year I shall have to watch for signs of young. If the elms keep dying, then the telescopes could even form the new metallic high-rise rookeries of the future. As dusk came the farmer in the next field began to burn stubble. The straw crackled as the flames leapt and smoke and smuts swirled into the wind. The sun began to set in a watery sky of high grey cloud, and again I finished the field quickly for:

> *If the sun goes pale to bed,*
> *'Twill rain tomorrow it is said*

And once more the old wisdom proved to be accurate.

When heaping bales up in Warners Corner, predation of an unusual kind took place, for Foss and Tinker both disappeared and left Nellie and Tirra looking for mice. I assumed that they had become bored and had gone rabbiting. Towards the end of the afternoon I noticed Foss slinking off by our neighbour's hedge, making for home; I whistled her, but she continued on her way and I assumed she had been frightened off by distant gun shots. When all the bales had been heaped I was standing by the hedge talking to our neighbour, when Tinker appeared. She had been rabbiting, for a black rabbit hung from her mouth; I shouted, her ears flattened, her tail went between her legs, she dropped the rabbit and ran off guiltily. Several of our neighbour's hutches had been ripped open and five rabbits were dead. I agreed to pay for the damage in corn, and I took two of the bodies back to eat. Tinker and Foss were chained up in disgrace.

It is fortunate that our Warners Corner neighbour is a friendly and tolerant man, as so many people who now live in villages do not fully understand farming life. But he could see the difficulties facing the dogs, for normally they are encouraged to flush rabbits from hedges, and so when confronted by rabbits in hutches, they could not believe their luck. He is an interesting man, who, in his younger days hitch-hiked with his wife around South America and South Africa, and during the course of his travels he picked up many skills. Now, in his long garden he grows strawberries, artichokes and various other vegetables, and rears rabbits and bantams. In addition he restores ancient engines, makes and engraves brass faces for grandfather clocks, and has a variety of crafts and occupations. On hot days he works stripped to the waist, showing a scar on his arm caused by a German machine gun bullet. He has nothing but contempt for politicians and union leaders who try to organise society, and they would not understand his independence; for he 'does his own thing', he thinks his own thoughts, and goes at his own pace, all of which are beyond the experience of most bureaucrats and party politicians.

In his garden there are a number of long established walnut trees, and this year they have yielded plenty of nuts. The trees were planted in the early thirties and have only just started to bear, for it is said that: 'He who plants a walnut tree expects not to

walnut

eat of the fruit.' Another saying is: 'A wife, a dog and a walnut tree, the more you beat them the better they be.' It is because of the walnut trees that an old villager says that the actual name of the field is not Warners corner, or Warns Corner, but Walnuts Corner, and that the real name has been changed by time and accents. Others disagree however, and there are no documents bearing the name Walnuts Corner.

In fact Walnuts Corner would be a better name, for not only is it now an accurate description, but it also has a pleasant country ring, and already Father uses it, claiming that he has never called it anything else. The field itself is fifty acres in size and for many years it was considered to be the largest field in the village. Over recent years hedges have been removed elsewhere, and now there are several that are even bigger. To look at it, it is rather ordinary, being flat clay-land, with the spinney at one side and a small grass field and the brook at the end. To politicians and townspeople however, the field is viewed only in terms of pounds per acre, capital-value, and wealth. But to working farmers, feelings for the land go much further than bank balances, and capital-value is quite meaningless. Each field is a place of memories and achievements, linked together by the progression of time. Over the years Warners Corner has been worked and improved and each new year adds to the catalogue of struggle, failure and success. There are still people in the village who remember gangs of men with scythes mowing it at harvest time, and then too it was ploughed by horses pulling wooden ploughs. Already my own memory records changes, as well as good times and bad. There were earlier harvests with binders, an old tractor and horses and carts. The threshing tackle in the winter, with village men on the stacks, the pounding drum, dust, noise, and rats and mice pursued by children and dogs. The old dressing machine used in the barns, shuddering and vibrating; tractors getting stuck in the mud while trying to plough, and a cold wet winter when the land was so waterlogged that all the sugar-beet had to be pulled by hand. A cow falling into a pit dug by workmen on a temporary builder's yard, and being pulled out by the tractor; hay cart; John cutting his hand on the needle of the baler; the cows in the corn; calves born in the long grass; good harvests; storm flattened crops; hares running, foxes hunting, hounds searching, and even geese flying over on a winter evening. Memories continue to be made; last year I found a leveret small enough to settle into my hand, fully furred with its eyes wide open, and this year the trailer turned over and there was the race to combine the wheat before the arrival of rain.

To us the field has no monetary value; it is a tool as well as our place of employment, where we work, rest, talk, take the dogs, pick blackberries, and see the procession of the seasons; we feel linked to it and a part of it, and any politician who wants to take it or tax it away, without our consent, is welcome to come personally and try.

But although the derivation of the name Warners, Warns, or Walnuts Corner is not clear, there are numerous names which have been handed down, and they simply describe old parts of the parish. There is Horse Field, Sparrow Field, Gnat's Close and Duck End, as well as many more. In addition there are old names for several of the local birds and animals, and many of them continue in everyday use. Snails are known as odny-dods, pheasants as longtails, foxes as Charlies or Reynards, hares as Sallies or Aunt Sallies, herons as heronshaws, little grebes as dab-chicks, fieldfares as fulfers, thrushes as mavises, hedge-sparrows as hedgie-betts, and pied wagtails as Charlie-Wags.

But the most appropriate names are the ones which describe wildflowers, for despite the efforts of botanists to make attractive plants seem totally unattractive, by insisting on using long Latin names, the old English names add interest and accuracy to the flowers they describe. The bristley ox-tongue and the bird's foot trefoil are two of the most aptly named, and both were on flower during the month. The bristley ox-tongue grows in waste places and resembles a large sow thistle; its name is perfect, for if a leaf is rubbed, it feels like a lick from the coarse tongue of a cow. In the same way the name bird's foot trefoil describes the plant exactly, for as the small yellow flowers die down and the seed pods develop, they look just like a bird's foot.

When honeysuckle is sucked, the 'honey' can be tasted, and it is also called woodbine because of the way it coils, climbs and binds in hedges and trees. Buttercup, goosefoot, and bindweed

bird's-foot trefoil

are others ideally named, while one of the best is the bee orchid. It is a beautiful flower, and each one looks like a bumble-bee surrounded by petals. Before the Second World War villagers could find these orchids in many meadows, and along the sides of the roads, but intensive farming, cutting, and the use of sprays have led to their virtual disappearance; now only a few odd plants remain in the rough ground at the bottom of somebody's garden.

Other names are just as straightforward and describe various plants in different ways. Fleabane was so called as it was once used to get rid of fleas, hogweed was fed to pigs, and when the leaves of soapwort were worked into water they made an effective substitute for soap. Similarly restharrow won its name when it was a common 'weed' in fields and pastures, for its roots and spiney stems stopped work when the harrows had to be cleared. The old names describe what was once obvious and they create interesting reminders of the past. The process is still going on, for during the last century Himalayan Balsam was introduced into this country from India. It has now colonised many areas, and because of the shape of its flowers it is widely known as 'Policeman's Helmet'.

The simple pleasure that flowers give can go further still, for many rural children once used them in their play to make daisy chains, cowslip balls, poppy dolls, and dandelion clocks. Grasses, burrs, hips and haws all had their uses and there were rhymes to say and things to taste and throw. Some children continue with the old flower games and there are still country looking lawns where daisy chains can be made. Unfortunately, in many homes such unsophisticated things are not encouraged, the toys are all plastic, the garden is out of bounds, and the simple delights of childhood are quickly put aside.

September saw the completion of three more harvests, one in the small orchard at the back of the kitchen garden, and two in the garden itself. All through the year we eat home grown fruit and vegetables, and although they do not meet all our needs, we are nearly self-sufficient. It is relaxing work, and unlike most gardeners I leave many weeds to their own devices; as a result scarlet pimpernel flowers are among the onions, groundsel goes to seed to attract the goldfinches, and sow thistles are allowed to grow as food for the pet rabbit. Even clumps of nettles are left, and earlier in the year we ate some as a green vegetable, after the pigeons had eaten all the spring cabbages. There were other difficulties too, for flea-beetles had many of the small germinating greens, and due to the season, whenever I wanted to sow it was too wet, and when I wanted to plant-out it was too dry, thus making it impossible to heed the old advice;

> *In gard'ning ne'er this Rule forget,*
> *For to Sow dry, and to Set wet.*

The dogs also like gardening, and as I work Foss usually lies close by, hoping that I will throw a stick for her to retrieve. When I pick strawberries or peas she is joined by Tinker, and they both eat what they can. They split or snap the pea pods and then eat the peas inside, and when they have nothing better to do they try the same with broad and French beans.

All through September we picked French beans; it was the second crop, as the slugs had the first. At one time the surplus beans were salted, but now they are cut up and put into the freezer. Marrows too were collected and the potatoes were dug up and

stored in paper sacks. During the same period I had to walk between rows of cabbages and brussels every day, for the abundant
butterfly summer had led to a plague of green caterpillars. I
picked them off in hundreds and threw them well away.

The other harvest in the garden involved seeds, for each year I
like to grow as many of my own seeds as possible. With vegetables like carrots and parsnips it means letting a few plants grow
into a second year, to flower and carry seed. Again they both did

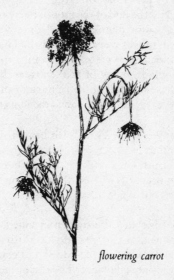

flowering carrot

well, and in addition I picked the ripe broad and runner beans,
left when the main crops were picked. Also this year I collected
lettuce seed, allowing one or two plants to 'run to seed', as I did
with radishes.

The fruit from the orchard was even more satisfying, as about
ten years ago I planted twenty-eight plum trees and four apple
trees. Since then we have picked nothing; most years the bull-
finches have stripped all the buds, although last year, when they
were absent, a late frost in May 'cut' all the fruit. I even tried
talking to the trees, encouraging them, and then threatening
them with felling, as some people advise, but it made no difference. This year after two mists in March, I gave up for:

There are as many mists in March as there are frosts in May

And I expected another fruitless year. One or two cold May mornings did follow, the orchard was left to become a miniature wilderness and the trees bore fruit. In early August I picked a large bucket full of Rivers, a deep blue plum with a taste as good as any exotic fruit, and others followed, including Victorias, Monarchs, and a large green plum that was awful to eat until cooked in tarts or pies. The Monarchs were as large as medium sized apples and by the end of the month the wasps were competing to eat them. Some plums we ate, some were bottled, some were frozen, and others were given away. The four small apple trees were also loaded, as were the Bramley trees in the garden. With the high winds, many of the 'cookers' became windfalls, and soon the house was full of the rich fruity smell of simmering chutney. It is easy to make and the mixture consists of:

3lbs apples	1lb brown sugar
1lb onions	½oz salt
½lb raisins	½oz ground ginger
¼lb mustard seed	¼oz cayenne pepper
1½ pints of vinegar	

The mustard seeds should be soaked in vinegar over-night and added to the minced or chopped apples, raisins and onions. The sugar and spices should then be added and cooked in a covered saucepan until they are all tender. The rest of the vinegar can then be added and the mixture allowed to simmer in an open pan until common sense says the consistency is right.

With the end of harvest, the harvest festivals were held on the last Sunday of the month at both the church and the chapel. The chapel was bedecked with flowers, dahlias, roses and asparagus fern, as well as a variety of vegetables, fruit, bread, packets of Ryvita, corn-dollies, rose-hips and jellies, together with wall posters comparing our plenty with the plight of the under-developed world.

For once there were no hops trailing over the clock, but there was a glass of water, a fortunate thing, for the preacher seemed to have the orthodox puritan view of alcohol. As he began, he admitted that he knew little about harvest or the country, and described himself as an 'academic'. As he went on the fruits of his extraordinary learning began to show: He implied that Jesus did not turn the water into ordinary wine, and that all large, strong animals of nature 'drink pure Adam's Ale'. As he spoke, my mind wandered for just as politicians and those hungry for power, make politics and the art of living, difficult, so many Christians and humanists, make simple spiritual truths and beauties incomprehensible.

Compared with the vegetables below the pulpit, I thought of a much more unusual display, for in the High Street old Albert had trained a trailing marrow up a tree. Consequently, six feet up and hanging with the apples were two fine marrows, and Albert's smile betrayed his pride. The thought of them was much more rewarding than listening to the profundities of an 'academic'.

October

Nature now spreads around in dreary hue
A pall to cover all that summer knew
Yet in the poets solitary way
Some pleasing objects for his praise delay

THE MONTH STARTED COOL and windy and on the first day, the first snipe of autumn flew up from feeding in the soft mud at the edge of the brook. A heron flew up too, on slow laboured wings, to settle in the stubble on the far-side. They often appear to stalk in the harvest stubbles, and like the foxes and kestrels they must take many beetles and mice with their long speared bills.

It was not a promising start, for on the second there was a slight frost in the early morning and it seemed as if winter was already setting in. Another spreadeagled hedgehog in the road showed that hibernation had not begun and the latest casualty made me wish that hedgehogs would develop razor sharp spines to puncture car tyres. The owners would then drive more carefully, although it would be a care for their pockets, rather than a genuine concern for life.

On the third there was no frost, with a cool mist filtering the sun's glare. Several pleasant days followed, with gentle light, soft colours and a mellow mistiness. The sky was a pastel blue, the leaves of the trees ranged from yellow, bronze, russet, and pale green, and the stubbles took on the look of new cultivation. Late bees were busy at the last roses and the scent hung refreshingly in the cool, still air. The bees were joined by tortoiseshell butterflies, which still found the hebes and michaelmas daisies attractive, while the wasps seemed to prefer the clumps of flowering ivy. One day two cock pheasants strolled arrogantly across the lawn by the back door at mid-morning, and Tinker looked at them with an expression of disbelief. But the 'conkers' fell from the horsechestnuts, reminding me of the true season, and the lapwings flew lazily in flocks, from field to field. Gulls too appeared in quite large numbers and one afternoon they jousted in aerial combat with the rooks over the spinney, but there seemed little urgency in their actions. At one time the appearance of gulls promised bad weather inland, for:

> Seagull, seagull, sit in the sand,
> It's never fine weather, while you're on the land.

But now, with several inland reservoirs quite near, many gulls spend their winters away from the sea.

On two mornings there was fog and dripping leaves, and in the second week the last of the swallows left. But in the main it was summer weather; the soil dried out and began to crack, and already by the eighteenth, St Luke's Little Summer had become a long and pleasant one. After the cold and wet of the spring, it showed again how the seasons almost invariably balance themselves out, for:

> Be it dry or be it wet,
> The weather'll always pay its debt.

With harvest gone we had our annual 'horkey', a 'blow-out' with food and homemade wine for all those who helped with the harvest, and Charlie discarded his beret and holey coat for a smart tie and blazer. With the immediate pressure of work eased, I even persuaded Father to have a rare afternoon off to watch the 'All Blacks' play rugby. The vicar and Robert the vet were also there, and as Robert walked by, a good humoured voice followed him: 'One week I seen him playing golf, the next watching rugby; no wonder my dog's always sick.'

During most nights the dogs woke us up with their barking, and foxes seemed to be the cause. On two mornings I saw a fox in the High Street, with an almost full grown cub sitting outside the Post Office and then sauntering off through a nearby garden.

After one night of barking a cockerel was dead and headless inside the hen house. Scratches on the glass window showed how the fox had jumped up and clambered through the small gap left for ventilation. The next night the furore started again and I had to roll reluctantly out of bed. Foss was furious and standing on her hind legs, trying to get a better view, and her eyes reflected pink in the beam of my torch. I slipped Tinker off her chain and she went charging off into the overgrown orchard, almost snorting in distaste, as she does when she gets the acrid smell of fox. As she blundered through the long grass and nettles I wandered along the roadway to the grassfield beyond, and there the fox sat without much alarm. As I approached it glanced casually towards me, its eyes flashing clear and bright, but its main centre of interest was the orchard, where Tinker continued to crash about in hectic hunt. The fox allowed me to get within thirty yards of it, as if sensing its own safety, before trotting off into the darkness.

'Bale cart' was finished and the land work started in earnest once more; but without rain the ploughed land dried out into miniature rock-hard boulders instead of crumbling into a fine seed-bed. The old horse-roller, long ago converted into tractor-roll, with numerous modifications, was in constant use, and in need of almost continuous repair. It was useless, and because of the conditions we decided simply to 'bust' the land with a sub-soiler, before harrowing and rolling in the hope that the soil would eventually break down to allow the drilling of the winter cereals to begin. The new tractor and its power steering took some of the effort out of the work, but after each day a bath was required because of the soot thrown up from the burnt stubble. One afternoon the conditions were perfect, with the sun streaming down to fire the leaves the colours of autumn. With the noise of the tractor at work, lapwings seemed to home in to the field, as if associating the steady drone of an engine working with easy feeding. When they fly they look black, white and distinctive, but when walking close to the tractor in the sunlight, their feathers shine with a brilliant green sheen that changes in its intensity with every movement. They have deep dark eyes, and with their upturned crest they seem gentle placid birds. One or two pied wagtails joined them bobbing, and searching the dis-

lapwing

turbed soil, and then black-headed gulls cruised in. They were already in their all white winter plumage and they wheeled over and behind the tractor before tumbling down to take worms or insects. Starlings and rooks made up the collection and Tinker sat patiently at one end of the field waiting for me to finish.

So the month continued to its end, warm and dry, as we battered the land and again repaired the rolls. But although the weather was unseasonal, Gypsy Jim was not to be misled, and in the last week, his waggons rolled by towards their winter campsite.

Early in the month a hundred and fifty pullets arrived, 'on the point of lay', and almost immediately small eggs began to appear. To make sure there were no problems on the first night, I was late to bed, in case the dogs started barking and a fox found its way into the deep-litter shed. But for once the dogs were quiet and just before midnight I decided to go to bed. It was then that a cow started bellowing in what sounded like pain and distress; the pitch was identical to that of a young heifer the previous year.

Then it had been her first calf, and after twelve hours of straining, with the calf still not showing, we had decided to calve her in the milking bale. Father had pushed his arm up to check the position, which had been normal but very tight. A piece of baler twine had then been tied round the front hooves, and John and I had pulled the other ends, with wooden handles passed through the loops to make hauling easier. Each time she had strained, we had pulled until the front legs had begun to emerge and the tongue and nose could be seen. But then everything had stopped; her skin would not give, and Father had not been able to ease it with his hands. Rachael too had joined the fray, but still the calf would not come. Again we had pulled and slipped and she had bellowed in pain, but slowly, fraction by fraction, the muzzle had appeared. She had strained once more, swaying and staggering, and for a second it had seemed that she would fall. Her balance had held, she had bellowed pitifully, and her udder had squirted milk through her teats because of the strain. Suddenly the head came and again she had almost gone down and more cries of agony came. Briefly progress halted, but then the calf had slipped out, and we had eased it onto the concrete floor, while drops of fresh blood joined the afterbirth with it. The calf had gasped and life had started; it had been a big animal and despite the pain and the trouble it had seemed like a miracle. John had then sprayed the umbilical cord with antibiotics, and then, as it had been a bull calf, he had rolled a large rubber band over its scrotum to cut the blood supply to the testicles, so ensuring that the little bull would quickly become a little bullock. It always seems a rather harsh birthday present, but until the sex of calves can be ordered with the semen, there is no other practical option. By the evening the young cow had still not accepted her calf, but in the morning it did not matter, for the heifer was just lying in the yard, as if resting, with no movement, and steam rising as heat and life left. On cutting her up for his hounds, the kennelman had found internal haemorrhage. All the suffering had been in vain.

With this memory still fresh, I slipped my boots on quickly, grabbed a torch, and ran to the yard, imagining another night of straining and struggle. I flicked the lights on, and there was a cow in the process of calving, with the front legs and nose of the calf already out as she stood in the corner. She bellowed with every effort, and with each strain the head showed, only to slip back inside. John arrived too, having been roused by the commotion. He slipped a rope over the front legs and with one strain and a slight heave the calf slid out onto the clean straw. It was a heifer; she took a deep breath and blinked. Almost immediately she sat up and started to look round at her new world. Her mother lowed softly and began licking the steaming wet coat of her off-spring. By morning the calf was walking on wobbly legs and had fed; there were no complications, no milk fever, and both mother and daughter were doing well.

It is with the return of the colder darker evenings that many of the village activities and organisations get back into their winter routines. In the lean-to by the Village Hall, the Mens' Club meets, whenever there are members who wish to play billiards or snooker, and several evenings each week, the lights, and laughter with muffled oaths show that a game is in progress. On Wednesdays there is often a queue to play, with games lasting from a few minutes, to over half an hour, when just the act of hitting a ball of the right colour seems to be a major achievement. On the second Tuesday of the month however, the language from the Club is always impeccable, for that is the night when members of the WI meet next door. Old Fred's wife has been a member for many years and he has got it all carefully worked out: 'They say WI stands for Women's Institute, but it doesn't, it stands for Women's Interference. That's right too; people say we're run by Parliament, but the country's been run by the Women's Institute for years.'

On the second Tuesday of this month over thirty women met together for 'A Favourite Recipe Evening.' A long table in the middle of the hall had been covered with a cloth and each new arrival added a dish or dishes to those already there. Most of those present were in dresses, but some wore trousers and one even arrived in jeans, showing how even the Womens' Institute is changing with the times.

Before tasting could begin, the business section of the meeting had to be completed, with the President and the secretary at the top table, and the ordinary members sitting, listening, and knitting woollen squares for an Oxfam blanket. Those with birthdays during the month were presented with birthday buttonholes, and then the business began with a variety of information; a dispute over the size of tins for a gingerbread competition had been successfully resolved; the stall at the Flower Show had made eighteen pounds, and there were vacancies for a shopping trip to Norwich. Those wanting to go to Oberammergau, in two years time, should put their names on a list, and there was news of a competition for a jar of fruit jelly, a child's birthday card, and a square for a blanket. The working knitting needles briefly halted when a cup was to be presented to the member gaining the most points at the Flower Show, but unfortunately the winner had been unable to get a baby-sitter, and had not arrived. Discussion then followed about *The Parish Guide*, which members had been updating for the Parish Council; a broad Yorkshire accent declared: 'A new-comer should do it, as they might see what we don't. such as letter boxes or Brownie meetings', evidently, despite her voice, she already regarded herself as East Anglian, and the others all nodded in complete agreement. The talk for the next meeting was announced as: 'My Twenty-one exciting days in South America', and the President asked for 'Any Other Business'. It then seemed that old Fred's fears about female domination were quite justified, for a new resident of the village asked: 'When is the Horticultural Society Annual General Meeting? I only want to know for my husband – are men allowed to go?'

The food followed and the women surged around the table enthusiastically to sample the cooking of others. The dishes ranged from 'Herb and Onion Bread', and 'Grandmother's Salad Dressing', to 'Courgette and Cheese Quiche', and 'Potage Parisien'. In fact there was such an array, that the less exotic samples at first went untried. Towards the end there was still a rather ordinary looking sponge cake left uncut, but to preserve harmony that too was sampled. The talk was of recipes, 'little Johnnie's measles', and the problems of running homes and families; but the women enjoyed it, and with the amount of food available, even old Fred would not have been dismayed.

By October, village football is also in full swing, and despite breaks when there was either no pitch, or no club, the parish has had a football team for many years. 'Training' is supposed to start at the beginning of August, but few people turn up unless a 'friendly' has been arranged with one of the neighbouring villages, and then summer idleness is quickly sweated off, as old scores have to be settled and new glories won.

It is strange how reputations for rough play, or hard games, spread from one generation to the next, and several of the old players watch each week. The game Charlie wanted to see more than any other was on the second Saturday of the month, for that was the day when we were due to play a team from the other side of the hill: 'They always used to be good local derbies against them. The best was when they hadn't lost a game all season and we hadn't won. We beat them one nil and we only got out of our half once; they didn't like that.'

The teams changed in the small pavilion on the recreation ground and trotted out; nearly all the home team are from the village, or have strong family connections with it. But as the referee blew his whistle to start, it was obvious that something was not quite normal; along one wing the grass was short, while over the rest of the pitch it was long and needed cutting. The answer was soon provided, as Rodney, the village postman and odd-job-man arrived on a tractor with the mowers at the back. He had started, stopped for dinner, and now was unable to finish; he pushed his postman's hat onto the back of his head and drove in a wide circle back to his car. Early on, the match had little shape, and it seemed as if the players had been watching too much football on television. There were 'sweepers' and 'front men' rather than 'forwards' and 'backs', and instead of being told to 'tackle', players were urged to 'close him down'. The visitors took the lead, but it was short lived, for after the ball had ricocheted around their penalty area, it hit a post and rebounded off the fullback's buttock and into the goal. Five more goals followed, and several were aided by the antics of the visiting goalkeeper, who seemed to concentrate more on diving through the air than on actually making contact with the ball, and twice he leapt spectacularly over it. The ball went into the ditch three times, and once when it rolled out of play, and the referee waved 'play-on', Charlie let the whole village know how he viewed the decision with a loud: 'Coorrd bloody hell'. A brief piece of excitement flared when one of their smallest players threatened our largest with an example of instant tooth extraction, but as local derby's go it was quite calm. They scored a consolation goal, and at 6-2 everybody seemed satisfied.

In the evening, sport of a different kind took place when the football club ran a 'disco' to raise money, by providing young people from several villages with their 'Saturday night out'. The hall rapidly filled with a variety of types and ages, from youngsters barely in their 'teens', to some of the Irishmen from the road. Several of the young men wore a single earing, the latest fashion and symbol of manliness. Drink flowed, the lights flashed and 'pop' music pounded out. The 'disc jockey', with long hair and wearing a suit, obviously enjoyed his 'star status', and like the footballers he had a clear image that he tried to project. Unfortunately his performance did not match his ambition, for whenever he announced a new record, his voice drifted over in an amplified blur, like a railway announcer on a foggy night.

Early on few danced, although two girls briefly danced in harmony, a new dance, full of explicit sexual movements. It was almost as if they were offering their wares for the night, but with cigarettes smouldering between their fingers and chewing gum vigorously, they aroused little interest. Gradually dancing began, and still more people arrived; it was the organised courtship display of homosapiens, and unlike the animal world with its specific mating seasons, most people seem to be in a state of almost permanent rut. Some drank, some danced, and one youth, on seeing a well developed girl dancing, muttered: 'Look at those knockers', and spent the night plying his lustful fantasies with alcohol. Halfway through the evening the 'bouncers' arrived, to prevent trouble; they were led by a large leather-jacketed youth in his twenties, and a short stocky man, almost as wide as he was tall, with tattooes over his arms. At one time they were often involved in disco brawls, but then somebody had invited them to become 'bouncers', to prevent trouble instead, and from then on the violence fell away. The evening reached its climax just before midnight; drink was drained, hands groped, and the disc jockey announced, so it was thought, the last record of the evening. Afterwards, the lights came on, the music stopped and the clearing up began. The crowd quickly dispersed, the 'bouncers' took their money, and the football club had made seventy pounds.

Throughout the month the hedgerows held their autumn beauty, with the leaves changing colour and the fruits ripening. The rose hips were plump and orange, and again I put off for another year my first attempt at rose-hip wine. The reason was simple, for there were so many blackberries that it seemed a waste of good time and fruit to pick anything else. An old country story claims that blackberries should not be picked after Michaelmas Day, 29th September, for the devil relieves himself over the fruit after that date, but I picked them all through the month. Although some got 'mushy', it was only where the insects and birds had joined in the feast, and blackberries usually remain good until a really hard frost.

There are many varieties, and I always visit the bushes with the biggest berries first, simply because they are so much easier to pick. Each year Sunday afternoon trippers come out from the towns 'blackberrying'. They came again this year, as early as August, but by the time the best stretches of hedgerow were ripe they had lost interest and had stopped coming. Several afternoons I went with a large basket and the dogs, and again when Tinker and Foss tired of rabbiting, they stopped to eat the lower berries.

Once blackberries have been picked there are many uses for them; they can be put into blackberry and apple pies, they can be frozen, made into wine, or boiled up into 'jelly', which can be used as jam in sandwiches, or as a pleasant medicine for bad throats in winter. It is easy to make, with common ingredients:

> 8lbs blackberries
> 2 pints of water
> 1lb of sugar for every pint of juice.

These are added to either the juice of three lemons, two level tea-spoonfuls of tartaric acid, or one pound of cooking apples.

First of all the fruit, water, and the acid or juice should be simmered for three-quarters of an hour. It should then be strained through a muslin bag and the juice measured. One pound of sugar is then added for every pint of juice and the mixture is boiled until the jelly will set when a small amount is placed on a saucer.

Although I did not pick hips during the month, I did make a special effort to find some sloes, and again they were few in number, despite the abundant blossom in the early spring. They are the

sloes

small, dark, sour fruits of the blackthorn, with the colour and the bloom of wild damsons; they too can be made into wine, but one of the most popular country drinks is sloe gin, which is a good cure for colds and flu. It is made with:

> One bottle of gin
> One bottle full of sloes
> and 1lb sugar.

The sloes are thoroughly pricked with a darning needle or a fork. Half of them, together with half the sugar, are then put in a bottle, which is filled with gin. The remainder of the gin, sugar and sloes make up the second bottle. The tops should be screwed down and the bottles turned upside down once a day until all the sugar has dissolved. By Christmas it will be a rich red colour and ready for drinking.

November

The village sleeps in mist from morn till noon
And if the sun wades thro tis wi a face
Beamless and pale and round as if the moon
When done the journey of its nightly race

IT CONTINUED MILD and fine and the ripe blackberries could actually be smelt along the hedgerows. The bristley ox-tongue, scarlet pimpernel, and even the round-leaved fluellen still flowered, as did the hedge bindweed, or bellvine, trailing its white bell-shaped flowers over hedges and walls. But the leaves began to stream steadily down, leading to some gardeners raking them into heaps and setting fire to them. I can never understand their desire for tidiness, for I enjoy seeing and walking through fallen leaves. Acorns fell from the oak trees and several times a rook flew over with an acorn or walnut in its beak. One morning a grey squirrel crossed the High Street with a nut carried in its mouth for its winter horde. Mice were also on the move and several came into the farmhouse. They gave themselves away by eating the apples, and a trap was set. One even installed itself behind a bookcase, feeding on ears of barley nibbled from a corn dolly. Neither Tinker nor the cats could catch it, but after three days it finally fell victim to the trap. I gave the body to Rusty, who greeted it with intense delight. She seized it, rushed around her run, and then flung it about like a ball, before eating it.

Yet another hedgehog was killed, and that night John heard a strange series of high-pitched whistles. It was a half-grown youngster and in the morning it was still there, making no effort to go. We assumed that it must have been orphaned and that its mother was the flattened corpse on the road. From its size it seemed unlikely that it was ready for hibernation, and so John adopted it; he applied a liberal sprinkling of flea powder, to get rid of unwelcome guests and took it into his house. The children named him Prickles and he quickly settled down, sleeping in a large box of straw, eating eggs, boiled or fried, ham, fruit, and the odd wood louse, and he washed them all down with fresh milk. In fact he settled in too well and had to be moved into a shed; he was a delightful little creature and it would be good to get him through to the spring.

The pullets began to lay a lot of small eggs and we sold many of them to Bert at the old shop for a penny each. His starting price was sixteen pence a dozen, but he could not sell them as people thought they were too cheap and that something must be wrong with them. As soon as he put them up to twenty pence a dozen they started to go: 'The trouble is,' he said, 'I can't put "Pullets' Eggs" up, because people don't know what they are anymore. I had a bloke come in here the other day and ask what they were. I said "pigeon's eggs". You should have seen him, he said: "Oh I've never tried them before", and he bought two and a half dozen.'

Cultivation continued in the fields and the drilling started, although it was still a struggle to break the soil down. One afternoon as I was rolling, the whole roller fell apart, with the draw-bar separating from the actual roll, and it took John over a day to repair it, with wood, wire, nails, and the welder. We desperately needed a long rain, the pond and the brook had dropped to well below their summer levels, and just inside the next parish a 'big' farmer irrigated some of his land with giant sprayers.

In addition to the land work, other jobs had to be fitted in; the cockerels were caponised, to make them put on more weight, and ten tons of artificial fertiliser, and eight tons of sugar beet pulp for the cattle had to be unloaded from their lorries in hundred weight sacks. The sugar beet pulp was the worst because the sacks were larger and made of paper, which were more difficult to grip. Williams came too, to test the heifers for brucellosis; it meant another morning of driving them into the cattle crush so that a blood sample could be taken from each animal. As he worked he confirmed that fox problems were quite widespread, and he told us of a call he had received recently from a woman who kept an animal refuge: 'She rescues anything, old battery hens, ducks, goats, and even her donkey was just a bundle of worms done up in a donkey skin when she had it. She would never shut up her hens and one night a fox went and chopped them down everywhere; when I told her the cause she just stood there nodding in disbelief, and so did the donkey.'

The foxhounds met in the next village on St Martin's day, the eleventh, but that was the one day which was foggy, cold and damp, and they didn't get far. The hunt catches a few foxes, but sometimes it seems that just the passing of the hounds drives them further away from the farms, or moves them on. However, it was a fine sight, with the horses and riders in the forecourt of an old pub. The hounds were eager to go and they were taller than some of the children they licked, who watched with wide eyes.

The real end to the drought came on the nineteenth, with the cars speeding past in clouds of spray. But the rain did not last long; normally in November it is said that the winter corn should be 'muddled in' on our heavy land, because of the wet, but in Horse field it was 'muddled in' because of the dry clods. More fine weather followed, and several times the rooks assembled at the rookery, and skylarks, robins, wrens, and blackbirds all sang. It often seems that territorial claims are settled in November in readiness for the spring. But the air cooled, the willow leaves spiralled down, and flocks of fieldfares appeared in the spinney and along the hedges of the brook meadows, searching for berries. Then came a series of wild sunsets, with vivid oranges, mauves, and pinks firing the high wisps of cloud in a lambent sky. A light fall of snow followed and then hard frost set in with the trees and grasses hoary white. In the frost John finished the autumn drilling, despite running out of seed, for Father dressed some of our own grain by putting the barley and the insecticide into a small cement mixer and churning them up. With the low level of the brook it quickly iced over, the puddles became solid, and every morning the drinkers in the cow yard and the hen houses had to be thawed out. On several occasions too even the milking machines had frozen. It was not a good omen, for:

> *If ice in November bear a duck,*
> *The rest of the winter'll be slush and muck.*

By the end of the month the ice would bear a duck, and on the brook it would almost hold me.

It is strange that the dogs dislike foxes, especially as they have all been used to Rusty, and tolerate her. Indeed, in the summer, whenever I called 'Rusty, Rusty', Foss rushed up to the run and tore round and round, making a well worn track. Occasionally I let her in to play, but I had to be careful, for a fox is still much smaller and more delicate than a border collie.

Foss had enjoyed the summer as she is a good swimmer, diving into the brook from the banks after pieces of wood, and each day as Father had shouted 'Come on. Come on', she would cut across Warners Corner to get the cows. On seeing her they would immediately head for the farm, and after snapping at the heels of the dawdlers, she would return ahead of them at full speed. She had been brave too, for several times, with hooves flying, she had tried to drive the bullocks, although in her excitement she often sent them in the wrong direction. If she had been trained properly she would have made an excellent cattle dog, but it did not matter for she had character and was a good companion.

It was because of the foxes that we decided to leave her loose at night. First of all we left Tinker unchained, but all she did was raid dustbins, and so she was chained up again and Foss was left to roam, in the hope that she would discourage the foxes, as we dislike setting snares. On the first night of her freedom I was woken up at two o'clock; she had been run over. Neighbours had found her whimpering and barking softly in the road, where she had been hit by a car and left. There was no blood, but she could only move her head, and the rest of her body seemed to be completely without life. Father fetched her home in the wheelbarrow and placed her in front of the Aga to keep warm. It was sad to see, and I had to fight back tears for we felt helpless and her eyes told of shock and fear. Rachael stayed with her, but I could not get back to sleep and after an hour I got up. She cried quietly as I went to her and licked my hand; I stroked her chin and spoke to her, but still she had no movement.

Despite her injuries, her spirit remained, for next morning she growled at a cat that went too near, and she snapped at the lady vet who came to inject her. We moved her under the kitchen table and put her carefully on a sack of straw, with a blanket and a hot water bottle for additional comfort. The vet said that movement might return and that we should wait two or three days to see what happened. We gave her tit-bits and glucose in water, and I kept imagining movement and a slight wag of her tail, but there was none. We tried to keep with her all the time, but when she was alone for just a few seconds she would whimper quietly until reassured. She could move her head perfectly, her eyes were bright and alert, and her ears responded normally. When people came whom she knew, her excitement showed, as if she wanted fuss, and they had to speak to her and stroke her. It was heart rending to see, for she showed trust and fear, helplessness and hope, yet there was no real way of consoling her, or of getting her to understand her plight. It was not until the second day that we realised one of her front legs was broken, but she could feel no pain. Tinker too knew that something was wrong, and anxiety showed in her eyes.

The lady vet came again and stuck a pin in various parts of Foss's body, but there was no response. She thought that the spinal cord must have snapped and there was nothing more she could do; she said that the only recommendation she could honestly make was that Foss should be put down, and Father, with grief on his face, reluctantly agreed. I stroked her head and talked to her as the needle went in and almost as soon as blood showed in the syringe, she was dead. I had expected her to tense up, or struggle, but as I comforted her she just stopped breathing; there was no fear and her life had simply been extinguished, like the flame of a candle. It was hard to take, for she had been as one of the family, and I cried like a child, tears streaming down my cheeks.

I carried her out and buried her under the apple trees, close to where she had often rested as I worked in the garden. It is strange how the physical act of digging helps to blunt sorrow. In the spring ground ivy will flower beneath the blossom of the trees and it is where we are going to plant some bluebells. Tinker was visibly concerned, and several times she went slowly and carefully to look into Foss's empty shed. For several days there were deep ripples of sadness on the farm, for familiar things were absent; there was no night-time barking, and the wagging tail, the bounding paws, the self-opening door, and the bright eyes wanting affection were all missing.

The end of Foss hung heavily over us all, for we get attached to our animals. This may surprise some people, as much farm stock is reared simply to die and we get used to death; but it is the needless waste of life which saddens, and this year the destruc-

Foss

tion of birds and animals on the roads in the parish had been as high as ever. In addition, each year over the whole country, thousands of people are killed or injured because of the car, yet the roads are made wider and the cars faster. It is clear from the carnage and the lack of care, that many who drive are both incapable and unsuitable, and it always puzzles me how so many hedgehogs can be run over, if the drivers are watching the road. The reason for the low driving standards is easy to see, for when many people try to play games or perform skills which require co-ordination between hand and eye, they just lack the natural ability to cope. Driving often requires much greater coordination than playing ball games, yet all those people who cannot hit a ball in or over a net are allowed to take control of a car after a simple test. Consequently the annual toll on the roads is hardly surprising. The number of people who drink and drive makes the situation worse, yet there is little legal deterrent, and if 'spot breathaliser checks' are suggested, then the motoring organisations talk about 'infringements of individual liberties', almost as if drunken drivers should have the right to put the lives of others at risk.

November was a sad month for another reason, for it seemed likely that because of Dutch Elm Disease, it would be the last season with the elms reflecting the sun in their autumnal shades of yellow. Already many were dead, but those remaining alive in the spinney, and beyond the orchard, were beautiful as their leaves seemed to linger because of the warmth; but it is doubtful whether they can survive much longer. It will be tragic if they die, for they are an important feature of our lowland landscape, although their appearance as a hedgerow tree is comparatively recent. Most of those in the parish date back to about 1840 when enclosure came and the land was divided into fields, with hawthorn hedges forming the boundaries, and elms were placed among them. The spinney was planted by a former squire of the village, and on the deeds of the house that go with it there is a prohibition on the lopping or felling of the trees; so what will happen if all the elms die will pose an interesting legal problem.

Being close to the farm, the spinney has almost seemed to be a part of it, and whenever the wind gets up we can hear it rushing through the branches. In summer, the breeze sounds like the surge of restless surf, and it gives the feeling of real country. Even the individual trees are attractive, with deeply grooved bark and an abundance of leaves that give good shade in hot weather and shelter in a shower of rain. Many times as a child I enjoyed picnics beneath them in the harvest field and memory always associates them with hot weather, stillness and buzzing flies. It must be accurate for it is said that:

> *When harvest flies hum,*
> *There's warm weather to come.*

I was high up in an elm when, as a youngster, I first saw some kestrel chicks; small fluffy balls in a hole in the trunk. The climb up the tree was memorable (even then elms had a reputation for danger as they always seem to contain a number of dead branches and stumps) for fear accompanied me all the way up. Jackdaws too love nesting in the holes, and the trees are a rich source of food for woodpeckers and many small birds. Elm wood has a pleasant texture and colour and for centuries it has been widely used by furniture makers. It is one of the most difficult woods to split, and for this reason it makes good chairs, and it was once used by wheelwrights for the hubs of cart wheels, as it did not split when the spokes were put in.

Dutch Elm Disease is now causing the leafless look of winter to remain the whole year through; it is a fungus disease and it is carried and spread by a small beetle. If the government, or local councils had acted swiftly by removing and burning dead trees, the epidemic could have been contained, but instead they moved with their usual lethargy, dictated by ignorance and bickering over who would pay if action was taken, and so nothing was done. 'Experts' say that the beetles came into the country beneath the bark of imported elms from Canada, despite port inspectors who are supposed to ensure that all foreign wood arrives stripped of its bark. As a result of this negligence, the whole countryside has been changed and is changing still.

The Parish Council, consisting of eight members and the Clerk, meets six times a year, and one of its meetings was held during the month in the village school, where already pictures of Father Christmas and reindeer were reminders of the approach of Christmas. There was an unusual start to the meeting, for the only woman member, Ruby, the doctor's receptionist, had put a pamphlet on every seat which read: DANGER: CIGARETTES CAUSE LUNG CANCER BRONCHITIS HEART DISEASE. Over the page it had snippets of advice for smokers such as: 'Do not inhale'; 'Take fewer puffs from each cigarette', and 'Take the cigarette out of your mouth between puffs.' Smoking is not allowed at meetings, and the literature distribution seemed designed to stir up Tom, an outspoken member of the Council who enjoys a 'fag'. It had the desired effect:

'I don't want one of these', he said, 'you read it', and he passed his sheet to Alfred.

'I will', replied Alfred, 'I smoke a pipe.'

'Yes, and what do you smoke in it, old socks that stink the place out worse than cigarettes.'

Norman, the Clerk, then began to read the minutes of the last meeting, which he had faithfully recorded. They have to be accurate, for Ruby is his wife and she would not allow herself to be misquoted. Once, when an increase in the clerk's salary had been discussed, Ruby had been the only one to vote against the proposal, saying that he received enough already; her view made the national press, and was then reported in newspapers as far away as Australia.

Following a request by the Council for a 'speed trap' to slow down speeding traffic, Norman read an apologetic letter from the police, stating how they would like to make the cars and lorries observe the speed limits, but they only had one piece of radar equipment for the whole area, which included two towns and the city of Cambridge. 'That's nice to know', Tom observed, 'that means it's safe to go as fast as we like.' The letter also caused much amusement for the 'speed trap' had been set up in the village the week before. It had been run by three cadets, with a bright yellow car, conspicuous white bands around their hats, and they had placed their equipment in an exposed lay-by which could be seen at least a quarter of a mile away; even so, five drivers were stopped, three were warned and two were prosecuted.

Fortunately there was better news from the police, for they had made enquiries and discovered that the drift used by the gypsies was an old 'green lane', and could be treated as part of the highway. The problem was, however, that according to the law, the gypsies could only be moved on if caught in the actual process of setting up their camp. Nevertheless, two policemen called on them and told them that another visit would be made to check the licences and insurances of their vehicles, and all the gypsies and didecoys suddenly left.

Most of the business was simple and was completed quickly; the Women's Institute had finished the Parish Guide, and the schoolmaster had agreed to print it. Nobody had any knowledge of an old ditch that had been filled in some years ago, and the Clerk reported that he had been unable to replace a memorial plaque on a seat outside the old people's bungalows. He had removed the screws of the old one, only to find that it had also been stuck on with glue, and would not come off. Tom mentioned that another seat was needed, and before deciding to defer a decision, in the best tradition of all councils, several minutes of discussion took place. Tom thought it was all quite senseless: 'By the time this council makes up its mind, half the people will be dead.'

'Then they won't have to use the seat, will they?' retorted Ruby.

Norman was having a busy evening, for he then read a letter stating that there would be no refuse collection during Christmas week, and finally he reported that the County Council had decided to change all the street lights to sodium, and that they would be triggered by photo-electric cells instead of time switches. There was little that could be done, for the decision had already been taken; it would mean that whenever it was gloomy the lights would automatically be switched on, and that they would also stay on all night. It represented yet another small erosion of the parish's rural character, for it seems to be the wish of planners and councillors to turn villages into comfortable suburban dormitories surrounded by country.

It is a fact, that for some reason, many villagers, particularly the newcomers, are afraid of the dark. When most of the street lights were switched off as an economy measure they complained bitterly, and the use of torches seemed to be beyond them. Yet despite all the talk about new street lights, the old 'parish lantern' was as bright as ever in the middle of the month, when there was a full moon. I enjoy walking around the fields in the moonlight, but I leave the dogs behind in the hope of seeing foxes. On the night I chose it was bright, with a far 'halo' around the moon warning of near rain, and for a few minutes cirrus and mackerel clouds briefly shrouded it with silver. By the barns of Warners Corner I startled a rat which fled for cover, and it is surprising how the darkness sharpens sight, sound and scent. Normally our senses must be working at a fraction of their real capacity, and the average office worker's 'reception' must be like that of a radio with the batteries almost run down.

As I walked, lapwings called and flew; they lacked the fear of daylight and simply ensured that a safe distance was maintained, before landing again. The hedges and furrows cast long shadows and everything had a silvery sheen, especially the leaves which looked almost as if they had been moulded in stainless steel; with the shades of white and grey against areas of shadow and total darkness, it was like looking at a series of pictures in negative. Along the brook a few rabbits were out, their tales reflecting brightly, and in the quiet, the warning thumps of their back legs were clearly audible. Pheasants flew from a hedge of blackthorn, and it was easy to see how they can be poached on a good moonlit night. The young cattle looked surprised to see someone about and they came over, sniffing and curious. In the grass field at the back of the farmhouse, the cows were lying down and some small birds seemed startled in a clump of brambles. A tawny owl hooted and flew silently by; their numbers appear to have fallen lately and they are now the only owls we see. I saw no foxes, and Tinker watched me return to the farm from the comfort of her kennel. The halo was still around the moon, and by morning a light rain was falling.

tawny owl

December

Christmas is come and every hearth
Makes room to give him welcome now
Een want will dry its tears in mirth
And crown him wi a holly bough

O N THE FIRST, it was still, cold, and frosty, but high cloud began to build up in the west, and it seemed that a thaw was in the air. I searched out my skates among several old pairs, including some ancient fen-runners, which at one time were

fen runner

strapped to ordinary working boots. Mine are screwed into a tattered pair of cricket boots, but they serve their purpose. The three dogs went with me down to the brook, and under the bridge where the water still flowed, two snipe flew up from their feeding. Further along, the brook was locked with ice, and cautiously I tested it, remembering the rule:

144

If it bends it breaks,
If it cracks it bears.

It cracked at first and for about fifty yards it held. It was pleasant gliding backwards and forwards, with the sound of metal on ice, the cold wind on my face, the warmth from my movement, and the spray of ice crystals when I stopped. Tinker and Tirra walked on the ice without fear, trying to run and appearing to enjoy the sensation of their legs moving with little control. A fox too had been on the ice, and had left evidence of its identity in the middle of a bend. Despite this, Nellie would not leave the bank; she barked and whined, and it was half an hour before she finally ventured on to the ice.

Because of the cold I moved Rusty to her winter shed, later than ever before; she was excited by the move, wagging her brush and diving into the fresh straw to play. But the thaw came during the night, with a warm wind, that quickly broke up the ice and things returned to normal. Father met a friend one morning who greeted him with: 'Oh I expect you've got nothing to do on the farm at this time of year'; it is the sort of comment we get accustomed to, and it is similar to those who assume that summer grass for the cows is 'free', simply because they have no knowledge of the expensive fertilisers and sprays that have to be used to make it grow. Heavy rain came and work fell into the routine of winter. The cows were confined to the yard, which meant extra feeding and 'strawing-up', morning and evening, and several had calves, which led to bellowing at night when they were separated. Feeding the calves with milk powder added to the work; slurry had to be moved from the entrance to the milking bale; sheds had to be cleaned out. John began the last of the ploughing, until the rain stopped him, and more wood had to be collected for logs. Father cleaned out a stretch of ditch by the farm, using a long handled shovel to throw the black mud onto the bank, and he also started to re-roof the old cowshed; stripping it of its thatch and replacing it with corrugated iron. It was a job that he did not really want to do, but the cost of re-thatching with reed or wheat straw made new thatch impossible. In any case, it is now difficult to get thatchers, as they are so few in number, and we have already been waiting four years for one to come and re-thatch the old granary. While he was up on the roof removing the bottom layer of reeds, Father found a crudely made mallet, which must have been covered up accidently when the roof was originally thatched. If so, the mallet is very old for the cowshed dates back to the eighteenth century.

Strong winds joined the rain and it was cold working in the mud and the damp of the farmyard. As Christmas approached the cockerels had to be killed and plucked for market and John, Father and Charlie, did most of them; they sat around a bath tub in the old cow shed, getting covered with white downy feathers. It was slow and tedious work and they were at it for three days. For the cockerels it was an unfortunate end and their brief lives had spanned just eighteen weeks. In that time they had put on as much as fourteen pounds in weight, and their bodies appeared to be almost too heavy for their gangling legs. This year too, several had died early; it was as if their hearts could not stand the rate at which they grew, and heart attacks resulted. It seems wrong that such birds should have been bred, but people don't appear to mind as long as they get their Christmas dinners reasonably cheaply, and they seldom pause to think about the morality of their eating.

Snow fell, but it soon thawed and the damp and gloom returned for the twenty-first, the shortest day of the year;

> *St Thomas grey, St Thomas grey,*
> *The longest night and the shortest day.*

On Warners Corner the winter barley germinated well after the rain, and by the fox's earth two fresh rabbit holes had been excavated. As I walked along the meadows, a large flock of lapwings settled by the brook, with several golden plovers among them, and there was one lone wader, with a long beak and a plaintive call. A family of goldfinches fed on the heads of the teasels and a party of long-tailed tits flew among the blackthorn; their calls resembled the brittle sound of the branches rubbing together in the cold wind.

Things changed for Christmas Day, which was clear and bright; it promised more fruit in the orchard next year, for;

Sun through the apple trees on Christmas Day,
Means a fine crop is on the way.

On the twenty-seventh I planted about two hundred bluebell
bulbs around the garden, as well as some small hazel trees, and
Father and Charlie put two maples in a hedge where Dutch Elm
had struck. Despite the earlier cold and the time of year, there
were a number of daisies on flower in the lawn.

As usual in the cold and damp of winter, the doctor was busy. I
got a virus infection, but he could give me no pills, and things had
to simply take their course. Mother gave me 'hot lemon', a mixture of lemon juice, honey and hot water, which she uses every
year to keep coughs and chest trouble at bay. It is surprising how
much of the old country medicine is still tried, even when modern drugs are available. Albert in the High Street recommends
the cool moist inside of broad bean pods for chapped lips, after
working on dusty land in the summer, and old Fred once had his
back covered with brown paper, which was then ironed with a
hot iron, to combat back trouble. According to Fred's own diag-
nosis he has been 'on the way out' for the last twenty-five years,
but at over seventy, he has not done too badly. During the summer, when grass cutting was taking place in the churchyard, he
leaned over the wall and said: 'I'll be in there soon', but 'creaking
gates hang long', and Fred seems to have enjoyed his years on
death's door. Perhaps his survival has been helped by his wife, for
she too is a believer in many of the old ways, particularly in bread
and milk as a protection against winter colds. She calls it a 'hot
milk mess' and pieces of bread, butter and sugar are covered with
hot milk; I suppose that as the mixture is fattening, it builds up
the body's insulation against the cold. Another well known local
winter remedy is for chilblains, when the feet of the sufferer have
to be bathed each morning in the chamber-pot; but although
several old villagers know of the cure, they all deny using it.

At one time both sickness and unemployment could cause
problems to those families affected, but now the Welfare State
assures that nobody comes to real harm. There are several unemployed people in the village, nevertheless they can still afford to

run their cars and drink in the local pubs.

In fact it is really surprising that unemployment is not considerably higher, for with technological advance we are now in the position where many people could be freed from work. Even in the village there is no real reason why milk should be distributed daily, and the letters could easily be collected, rather than delivered. Machines and computers could also replace many jobs, leading to earlier retirements or a much shorter working week. But the brains of the politicians and union leaders cannot cope with the new attitudes required, or the new opportunities, and they still proclaim policies of 'full-employment'. They assume that people should be happy doing repetitive, senseless, or thoroughly worthless jobs, even if machines could master them far more easily. Indeed it could be that the motorway skirting the village was really planned to create jobs, for it is not really wanted. Yet thousands of men have been involved in the work, and the machinery used has also created jobs for others; I wonder what they will do when they run out of suitable land to cover with roads or concrete? Perhaps they will build dams and flood the rest.

The Cambridge Cattle Market takes place every Monday; at one time it was always full of animals, but now with the decline of mixed farming in the area, many of the pens are empty, although farmers continue to attend, almost out of habit. I went on the second Monday of the month, when the annual fatstock show was held, and prizes were awarded for the best animals.

Around the refreshment caravans, selling tea and hot pies, groups of elderly farmers assembled, with long coats, rosy weathered cheeks, and cheap cane walking sticks. They are a dying race and their whole bearing reflects the ages and hardships that they have lived through; when many of them walk they take long slow strides, almost as if they have still got heavy clay caked to their boots, and it would be possible to tell their occupation anywhere. When a handbell was rung the 'Produce Auction' began; it was held in a shed with eggs, apples, pears, cockerels, pheasants, pigeons, Brussel sprouts, Christmas trees and turkeys, all for sale. The old auctioneer, with a cap over his eyes and a sheet of paper in his hand, called for the first bids, and even older men in white coats shuffled about making sure the successful bidders paid their money and received their goods. In the middle of a burst of bidding for apples, one of the white clad helpers loudly reprimanded a bidder with: 'Don't tell me your bid, I'm not the auctioneer.'

Elsewhere other trade went on, and in a dark, damp building, rows of junk were all numbered ready to be sold later. There was dirty second hand furniture; marked and cracked, a bent old soldering iron, that had to be placed in an open fire for heat; damaged mirrors that reflected no image; and a very old upright mangle in working order. Outside, the bicycle auction was in progress, and again it was rubbish, with buckled wheels and worn saddles and fifty pence seemed to be the average price. It was a strange trade, but apparently undertaken seriously by those doing the bidding. A few van drivers were present selling nuts, bolts, wellington boots and farm clothing, and one had sacks of black-soiled vegetables, with a red-faced couple sitting outside, urging: 'Buy all your winter vegetables here. Grown in the Fens at the cheapest prices; carrots, sprouts, parsnips, and potatoes.'

Around the livestock pens men came and went, as did numerous cattle trucks. To make some pigs walk down the ramp, one driver twisted the tail of an awkward animal; it made me smile, for a few days earlier I had heard a lady on the radio, complaining in a cultured, affected voice, of the export of live animals to Europe. Horror of horrors, she had seen a Frenchman twist the tail of a calf to get it into the lorry. She had evidently not been to many English markets, and she simply eased her own carnivorous conscience by blaming 'foreigners'. Unfortunately the movement of live animals anywhere involves hitting, twisting, or cajoling, whether it is in France or England.

When another handbell sounded, the pig auction got into full swing, and the auctioneer gabbled off figures and facts in a way that outsiders would never understand. At the sheep, old men lent over the railings of the pens and dug their fingers into the fleeces, to feel the bodies underneath; while at the cattle there were knowing nods, prods and pats. The animals were in superb condition, with some clipped along the back for the benefit of the judges. It was difficult to distinguish the breeds, for many had been crossed with big-bodied foreign animals; the largest was almost as tall as me at the shoulder, being a cross between an English Red Devon and a French Blonde Aquitaine. It was not in the show, but in a 'guess the weight' competition run by the auctioneers; the prize was a gallon of whisky.

The poor beast had a lot of meat on it, and there is no doubt that roast beef and horseradish sauce make an excellent meal, and that, of course, is the prime concern of markets. Horseradish grows wild around the farm and in the garden, and when we want it, we dig up a root and use it while it is fresh. The simplest sauce is made by adding fresh horseradish to some milk, sugar, and vinegar, according to taste. My grandmother's old recipe is a bit more specific however, with:

> 4 tablespoonfuls of grated horseradish
> 1 teaspoonful of castor sugar
> 2 teaspoonfuls of made mustard
> A little salt and pepper
> A gill or more of vinegar (a gill is a quarter of a pint).

The ingredients, except the vinegar, should be well mixed and then covered with cream and stirred. The vinegar should then be added and the whole mixture thoroughly blended. Finally it should be heated, but not allowed to boil. The easiest way is to place the sauce container in a saucepan of boiling water.

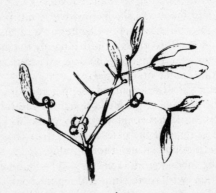

mistletoe

Throughout the month there was a steady build up towards Christmas. Decorations appeared in the village post office, and in the pubs, to encourage customers to part with their money, and others appeared in the village hall, simply to engender the feeling and spirit of Christmas. Yew and laurel were fixed to the beams, as were ribbons, tinsel, large cardboard Christmas crackers, and pictures of Father Christmas. Some people also had their own supply of mistletoe at the ready, and kisses were offered and accepted.

A series of parties followed, with the Bowls Club Dinner, the WI Christmas party, and the Horticultural Society party. The Horticultural party has become very popular, for numerous bottles of homemade alcoholic punch and home-brewed beer appear, and inhibitions completely vanish; they eat well and play traditional games such as musical chairs and musical parcel, with an enormous parcel, as well as modern innovations, such as passing Polo mints on cocktail sticks held in the mouth. Towards the end of term the village school presented its annual concert, in front of parents and friends, and the story of the nativity was told, acted and sung. It had one slight change from the Biblical version, for one of the angels, in spotless white, developed a nose bleed. At the White Horse, the annual draw was held, when many prizes were won, food was produced, and an open darts competition took place.

In the house the smell of seasonal cooking permeated the atmosphere as mince pies and cakes were made in readiness for the festivities, and a large ham was cooked. Carols were played on the radio and a small group of carol singers visited the homes in part of the village. At last the true message of Christmas seemed to be seeping through, and there was anticipation in the eyes of the children and smiles on the lips of the people. A carol service was held at the church, and then at the chapel, and on Christmas Eve the church was full for Midnight Communion; it seemed as if some of the congregation might have taken the wrong turning after leaving the Hoops, for faces were seen that never appear in the church at other times of the year; but the setting and the singing were just right for Christmas, and it was enjoyed by all. The new vicar is popular at the moment, but he should take care, for an old saying warns of the fickleness of many parishioners:

The first year they eulogise,
The second year they criticise,
The third year they scandalise.

Christmas is a time of genuine goodwill, when the message of the first Christmas competes with the material affluence of a comparatively godless age, and for a few days, in many homes, it seems to win. In the High Street there is a fine old countryman, who for many years worked on the land, and who has always been a regular church goer. For a recent Christmas he wrote a poem for his grandaughter, about a donkey that could be seen from the bridleway to Grantchester, before the motorway intervened. He called it *The Story of Donkey Fred*, and in it he shows both the spirit of the season and of the countryside:

Old Fred he stands with downcast eye,
He shakes his head and wonders why,
This empty meadow for my home
And I stand sadly here alone.

He calls to mind a summer day
And folk who walked the Bridleway,
Who stayed awhile and had a chat
And gave old Fred a friendly pat.

He wonders if it's true, that when,
A donkey went to Bethlehem,
That Mary on his back did ride
With Joseph walking at her side.

And now the stars are shining bright
And darkness falls, once more 'tis night,
Now all is quiet, and donkey Fred
Walks slowly to his humble shed.

And underneath the starlit beams
Old Fred the donkey sleeps and dreams,
With shepherds poor and the wise men
He walks the road to Bethlehem.

152

And one bright star looked down and led
Old donkey Fred to Jesu's bed.
He lowly kneels and with a bray
Greets Jesus Christ on Christmas Day.

And Mary said, we thank you Fred
For coming to our manger bed,
Tell folk who walk the Bridleway,
You came to us on Christmas Day.

On Boxing Day, John wanted to walk around the fields after pheasants, as Boxing Day shoots are traditional and go back many years. The very fact that he wanted to shoot shows the strange relationship between country people and pheasants. During the summer, the sight of a hen bird and her brood leads to protective feelings and pleasure, but in winter it is different, and the pheasant is seen as a welcome addition to the dinner plate.

He wanted to take Tirra and Nellie with him, although Nellie had never seen a gun before, but he suggested that Tinker should be left at home, as she seems to think that pheasants and rabbits are propelled from the barrels of guns. Normally when I go for a walk, carrying only my ash stick, cut out of the hedge, she works busily in search of rabbits and game, but as soon as a gun is present she runs excitedly about, with frequent stops to look at the barrels, with ears up in expectation. We decided however, that at twelve years old, her stamina and enthusiasm might have waned and that she would be easier to control.

Because of the drilling and the farm work it was the first shoot of the year, and during the month I saw several pheasants, groups feeding on the ploughed land in the early morning, and others going up to roost in the spinney and the blackthorns of the jungle at dusk. I do not usually shoot, but for once I took Father's old double-barrelled shot gun, with just one hammer, hoping to get a dinner. Rain during the night had not made things too promising, but as we moved off we were joined optimistically by a Swedish visitor, and a bearded Scotsman who had recently moved into the village, bringing a broad highland accent with him.

The land was heavy on Warners Corner and picked up on our boots; Tinker was not interested in our neighbour's rabbit hutches on this occasion, but ran around excitedly from one gun to the next. Tirra was much better behaved and stayed with John, and Nellie followed me, not knowing what was going on. We spread out and walked across the field. I was supposed to be encouraging Tinker to work a hedge, but she wasn't interested, still expecting a magic gun to fire a pheasant at her. Two hares ran off, but they were out of range; I was glad, for I dislike seeing hares shot, and in any case their numbers are still low. Down in the brook meadow, Tinker briefly stayed with me, but when John shot a rabbit, she was off, and sure enough the magic had worked again. Near the jungle a cock pheasant flew up and I shot it as it was halfway across the brook. It was the first pheasant I had ever shot at; it fell dead, but its momentum carried it to the far bank. Tirra and Tinker both arrived on the scene, swam the brook, smelt the pheasant, and swam back again, leaving the bird where it was. The water was quite high and it meant that if I wanted the pheasant I would have to get wet, as the brook was too wide to clear. I jumped at the narrowest point, clearing the deep water, but still getting wet well above the knees. It was icy, but I got back safely, as the dogs watched with interest; it is a pity that their enthusiasm for retrieving bits of wood cannot be transferred to pheasants.

When a flock of ferrel or racing pigeons flew over, several shots were fired, as our brains simply registered 'pigeons', but none were hit. Despite the fact that shooting racing pigeons is illegal, I would not have felt guilty, as some pigeon fanciers break the law and kill many hawks and falcons, including the magnificent peregrine falcon, simply because they eat a few pigeons each year. Nellie did not like the shooting, and after every shot she cowered nervously. When two shots were fired simultaneously she turned tail and went home. Walking along the brook meadows in the bright sun talking, working off our Christmas food, and watching Tinker still running about almost like a puppy was pleasant. She proved her worth however, for when a pheasant was winged, she dived into some brambles and killed it quickly. A small covey of partridges got up, but again they were out of range; if they had been nearer, I would not have shot as they had experienced a poor breeding season, and in any case I prefer just to see them.

Altogether we got three rabbits and three pheasants, and although I do not really like shooting, it meant rabbit pie and roast pheasant, which is far tastier than Christmas turkey or cockerel. Whenever we have game, chicken or rabbit, we start the meal with 'light pudding', a savoury dish which seems to settle the appetite perfectly. It is a pudding that mother makes using a recipe that was handed down from her mother, and it has never even been written down. It should be served with plenty of thickened gravy, and the ingredients for a pudding to serve between six and eight people are:

> 8ozs of self-raising flour
> 1 teaspoonful of baking powder
> 3 ozs of margarine
> 2 eggs
> Milk

The fat has to be rubbed into the flour and then the beaten eggs should be added and mixed in. Finally milk should be poured in and the consistency should be quite stiff, and certainly not runny.

The mixture should be baked in a greased 'Yorkshire pudding dish', for twenty minutes, until it has risen and the top is crisp; alternatively it can be steamed for an hour and a half.

On the last day of the year, bleak weather set in, meaning that for once the old weather lore was wrong, as the 'mud and slush' froze solid. Snow came and the temperature plummeted; but I enjoyed it, and in the spinney the dogs flushed three cock pheasants, whose vivid colours were exaggerated by the backcloth of white. The brook flowed fast again, and had no ice, and among the undergrowth of the banks, small birds sheltered with their feathers ruffled because of the cold; even a snipe seemed to be feeling the effects of the freeze-up, for it flew with unusual lethargy. Darkness came, the temperature fell still lower, and several days of cold seemed likely.

The year closed with the family in front of a log fire, some with glasses of sloe gin, which more than compensated for the cold outside. As usual the old year had been full of both the predictable and the unexpected; with humour and sadness; hard work and times of enjoyment; quiet and contemplation. Life will still go on around the farm and in the parish, and I hope to continue to walk with my stick and the dogs over familiar land. But more changes will come as time passes and the future is unknown and uncertain. My hope is that others in years to come will still be able to enjoy the simple country life, and draw pleasure from the wild creatures and plants that should share it with them. My fear is that it might already be too late.

Index